writing the research paper

Revised in accordance with the second edition of the MLA Style Sheet

Neal Frank Doubleday
Millikin University

D. C. HEATH AND COMPANY
Lexington, Massachusetts   Toronto   London

Acknowledgments

Grateful acknowledgment is made to authors and publishers of the following works for permission to use these selections.

From John William DeForest, *Miss Ravenel's Conversion* in *Secession to Loyalty,* Rinehart Edition, edited by Gordon S. Haight, 1955. Reprinted by permission of Holt, Rinehart and Winston, Inc.

From *A Volunteer's Adventures* by John William DeForest. Edited by James H. Croushore. Copyright © 1946 by Yale University Press. Reprinted by permission of the Yale University Press.

From *American Poetry and Prose,* edited by Norman Foerster. Reprinted by permission of the publisher, Houghton Mifflin Company.

From *Witchcraft in Old and New England* by George Lyman Kittredge. Reprinted by permission of Harvard University Press.

From "Air Pollution and Public Health," by Walsh McDermott. Copyright © October, 1961, by Scientific American, Inc. All rights reserved.

From *The Colonial Mind 1620–1800* by Vernon L. Parrington. Reprinted by permission of Harcourt, Brace & World, Inc.

From *The Theory of the Leisure Class* by Thorstein Veblen. All rights reserved. Reprinted by permission of The Viking Press, Inc., and George Allen and Unwin, Ltd.

Library of Congress Catalog Card Number: 68–17701

a note to the instructor

When it was suggested to me that I do a book on source paper writing, I thought it might be an arid task. But I have not found it so. Rather I have enjoyed the reconsideration of problems that I had encountered in the classroom, in editing controlled research texts, and in writing literary studies. I hope this book offers the textbook help that students writing source papers most need — help in the handling of the sources themselves.

Two difficulties are inherent in the task; both will be familiar to the instructor from his own classroom experience. One is that any matter of composition instruction is conceivably applicable to source paper writing. But no book should try to do everything, and this book considers matters of style and structure only in their particular applications to the source paper. The other difficulty is that textbook and instructor must deal with one matter at a time, and yet try to keep the instruction ahead of the students' need for it as they work on their papers. The instructor may wish to determine the order in which the chapters are to be used to fit the needs of his class.

It is assumed that the students will have had some practice in the writing of formal summaries or précis. If that is not true, it may be well for them to have that practice before the source paper instruction begins or early in it, for the formal summary is a useful preparatory exercise. And it seems to me a good procedure to have students do some exercises in the use of sources or a short source paper before they do their major papers, so that misapprehensions may be discovered before they do very much harm. A good many students seem to require the chance to be wrong once.

In matters of style, this book follows the second edition of the *MLA Style Sheet* with only slight and infrequent deviations appropriate to papers written by undergraduates. I have tried to ascertain and to illustrate the best contemporary practice. Parenthetical documentation is fully discussed and illustrated. But I have avoided the discussion of forms for which students have no possible use. Above all I have tried never to suggest that external form is all that matters in a source paper.

A good many source paper topics are assumed for purposes of illustration, but of no one sort; and the book may be used with a controlled research book or without one. I believe that lists of miscellaneous source paper topics make the wrong sort of suggestions to students, but perhaps some of the example passages will lead some students to topics that will interest them.

This is a "show and tell" book. I am quite aware of the risks of trying to show, but I believe that they are risks that must be taken if a textbook in source paper writing is going to give students help where they most need it. I have used a few passages from my *Writer to Reader* (D. C. Heath, 1966) in this book, since there is evidence that they have helped students in their papers.

N. F. D.

table of contents

1 the source paper: first considerations

Writing a documented research paper or source paper, in which the student investigates an assigned or chosen subject, is an important part of the work in a good many college courses. Presumably you are about to write your first such paper in college, and the task may seem to you somewhat forbidding. It is true that any paper worth the writing offers its own problems, but the problems are not, fortunately, always new. There are ways of approach, ways of handling sources, conventions of documentation, and principles of structure that, once you understand them, you can use in a variety of source papers. It is the purpose of this book to show you how to work with sources and to write the source paper.

Source papers may be written in many fields, but a good paper in any one of them requires, first of all, a careful consideration of a substantial body of information, and then a selection from that information, organized and interpreted for a precisely defined and limited purpose. Problems will have to be discussed one at a time, but they can be taken up here approximately in the order the student writer encounters his problems. This chapter considers in a preliminary way the relationship of the source paper to its readers and defines kinds of sources; then it discusses the choice of topic, and the determination of the sources. Subsequent chapters deal with the ways in which sources are used, with the documentation of the paper, and with its organization.

The Source Paper and Its Readers

Any piece of writing has its function and its life when someone reads it. If that is not remembered in the writing of a source paper, the paper becomes a sterile exercise. Now one of your readers is your instructor, and admittedly it is he who will make a judgment of your paper. But he does not necessarily want you to envisage him as your reader. For one thing, he may know as much as you do about the topic of your paper. For another, he stands in a special relationship to you, one that is not paralleled in any other reader. And in any kind of writing (except some academic exercises) the writer writes because

1

he believes that he can inform or enlighten his readers. No one who disregards the very purpose of writing can write well.

It will not be difficult to envisage the sort of readers for whom you can write. You should assume competent readers with some initial interest in your subject—without that initial interest no one is likely to read a research paper of any sort. You might assume like-minded classmates as your readers. Since these readers have an initial interest in your subject, they will know something of it —perhaps just about what you knew when you began your work. But of course they will not have read what you have read in preparation for your paper, nor be able to think about the topic in the context you have acquired. You will need to remember that, and to avoid the unconscious assumption that the reader has read what the writer has. Student writers can easily fall into it, since they so often in exercises, examinations, and reports do write for instructor-readers who know more of their subjects than they do.

You will need, then, constantly to ask yourself as you write, "Will this be clear to my reader?" Indeed, you should also ask, "Have I given my reader any chance to misunderstand?" These are, of course, questions any writer needs to ask himself; for the writer of the source paper, they have some special applications. In the first place, the worst mistake the writer of a source paper can make is to misinform his reader about what a source says. That mistake may be a matter of careless statement; very often it goes back to a misreading of the source. Moreover, if the writer forgets that his readers do not have the same context he has gained in his reading, he may mislead them—not by any actual misstatement, but merely by not providing adequate context for what he draws from his source. In the second place, the writer of a source paper has a responsibility to make entirely clear to his reader the relationships between his sources and his paper. That is something most college students have to learn to do; a good deal of the subsequent discussion in this book will be concerned with the ways in which those relationships are made clear.

You may feel that you need some illustration of the writer-reader relationship in writing done from sources. It will, of course, be illustrated within this book, but you might do well also to examine the work of some professional writers at the outset. In their length and in their strictly limited purpose, articles in learned journals are close to what you are being asked to do, and you might examine some articles in *American Literature*, say, or *The Journal of American History*. But with the articles in such journals you must remember that the writers are assuming a considerable knowledge of their subjects on the part of their readers. The articles in *American Heritage* and the profiles in *The New Yorker*, although undocumented, are better examples of the sort of writer-reader relationship you will wish to achieve.

But perhaps it would be more profitable for you to read parts of two or three scholarly, documented books: studies of subjects of interest designed, not for a general public, but for a fairly wide public. Your instructor may wish to suggest such books to you; or you might use some of the scholarly works mentioned for illustrative purposes in the course of this book. Of these, three seem particularly useful examples: Louis C. Hunter, *Steamboats on the Western Rivers* (Cambridge, Mass., 1949); Ronald E. Shaw, *Erie Water West* (Lexington, Ky., 1966); and James D. Hart, *The Popular Book* (Berkeley, 1961). The books by Hunter and by Shaw are documented, and Hart's "Bibliographical Checklist" is so full that it constitutes a form of documentation. If you will watch skillful professionals handling their sources, you can learn a good deal about how it is done. Of course what you write will have a much more limited scope.

Primary and Secondary Sources

It is important to distinguish two classes of sources. A primary source is a piece of writing with the most immediate sort of relationship to its subject matter. In the field of history, primary sources are journals, state papers, letters, newspaper reports, and many other kinds of records. Secondary sources are works with a less immediate relationship to their subjects, and often considerations of a number of primary sources worked into a pattern. What are called histories are secondary sources (unless they are written by persons who lived through the events described). For example, in a study of the Salem witchcraft trials of 1692, the records of the trials themselves, Cotton Mather's *Wonders of the Invisible World* (1693), and Robert Calef's *More Wonders of the Invisible World* (1700) are primary sources; George Lyman Kittredge's *Witchcraft in Old and New England* (1929) is a secondary source. In a study of Hawthorne's *The Scarlet Letter*, the romance is *the* primary source; critical interpretations of the romance, and books and articles about Hawthorne's life and work are secondary sources.

Yet the distinction between primary and secondary sources is not absolute; it is relative to the kind of subject being discussed. If one were writing a study of the reception of *The Scarlet Letter* in Hawthorne's own time, contemporary reviews and references to the book would be primary sources. Or, for an undergraduate doing a study of the relationship of *The Adventures of Tom Sawyer* to Mark Twain's own boyhood experience, Dixon Wecter's *Sam Clemens of Hannibal* (1952), which uses materials unavailable to undergraduates, might have a sort of primary status. Again, Henry Adams' *Mont-Saint-Michel and Chartres* (1904) would be a secondary source for a paper concerned with medieval cathedrals, but a primary source in a study of Adams' thought.

Your instructor may wish you to confine yourself to primary sources. Or he may wish you to use primary sources properly supplemented by secondary sources. Rarely, with some special projects, particularly when primary sources are unavailable to undergraduates, the use of secondary sources alone may be justified, but not the extensive use of such secondary materials as encyclopedias and textbooks. In most college courses it is taken for granted that no student will write on a subject unless he can read and understand the material basic to it. For instance, he will certainly not write on some development in medicine or pharmacology if he is able to read only the repetitious articles on it in mass magazines.

Choosing a Topic

Topics for source papers in upper division courses will have a close relationship to the instruction in the courses, and perhaps the topics for source papers in composition courses will too. But in any source paper, you will do well to choose a subject on which you have a little background and interest, or, failing that, to provide yourself with background before you try to determine your concentration. If for instance, you want to write on early American railroads knowing little about them, you might read some general study, perhaps the appropriate parts of George Rogers Taylor, *The Transportation Revolution 1815–1860,* and gain enough background to find out what you want to do (as well as some sources useful to your purpose). You need to know something in general about a subject before you can make an intelligent choice of a workable concentration within it.

As soon as possible, you need to find a limited purpose for your paper, one that you can define clearly and carry out within the assigned length. You may have the help of your instructor in defining the concentration and purpose of your paper. Yet you will need to think about the matter for yourself too. If a topic you hit upon is a possible subject for a big book, it is clearly not a possible topic for a relatively short paper. But that obvious truth in no way precludes your writing within your interests. If you are interested in, let us say, the history of railroads, you can define some segment of the subject that you can handle with reasonable thoroughness in the limits of your paper. You clearly cannot write on "Railroads in the United States"; but you may well write on how the railroads brought about the end of the canal building era, or on the first diesel locomotives, or on any other manageable segment of your interest.

Likewise, if you are interested in the work of a novelist, you cannot discuss all of that work entire; but you can write on the special excellence of one novel, or on one of the novelist's particular qualities as it is exhibited in two or three novels. Indeed, your concentration might well be much narrower than either of those. You might discuss the way in which the novelist deals with a single character, or the narrative-point-of-view in one novel.

It seems almost inevitable that a student's interests lead him into too big a subject at first. A student is likely to go through some such process as this: His general interests are, let us say, technical, and he may have a little familiarity with and interest in canal building in the United States. He decides, therefore, that he will write a paper on the engineering achievements of the canal building era, and he hopes that he has established a manageable topic. He soon discovers that his topic is far too big; he will, he thinks, limit himself to the engineering achievements in the construction of the Erie Canal; and with that much limitation he starts to work. But before he has gone far, he will — if he is thinking clearly about his problem — come down to concentrations something like "The Locks at Lockport, New York" or "Canal Construction in the Montezuma Marshes." If he considers both of these concentrations, he may fix upon the one for which he can find the most usable source material.

Determining the Sources

When you have chosen a topic, you will probably have in mind two or three pieces of source material, primary or secondary, to start with. You will need more — but not a great number. It is far better to have a few well chosen sources than a large number gained merely by picking out likely-sounding titles from a subject index in a card catalog. In many undergraduate papers, the primary sources are no problem; they either are given as part of the assignment or are what must be known before the topic can be chosen at all.

But of course a student's initial interest and information may come from a secondary source. Now that source itself may lead him to the primary sources; if it does not, a scholarly book on the subject will. Indeed, you may find one source leading to another, and the second to more, so that you will never have "to make a bibliography"; your sources will have gathered almost of themselves. Let us suppose you are contemplating a paper on conservation, your interest having been awakened by your reading of Stewart L. Udall's *The Quiet Crisis*. That book itself will suggest a number of topics and some sources; and it will furnish a good general context for your thinking about almost any topic on conservation in America. If the work of John Wesley Powell turns out to be the topic that attracts you, *The Quiet Crisis* will lead you to an excellent book on Powell, Wallace Stegner's *Beyond the Hundredth Meridian*. But before you make use of it, you will want to find the names of Powell's chief works (you can do so in the *Oxford Companion to American Literature*) and make sure they are available to you. If so, you have enough to get on with, at least until you have found your concentration on the topic.

But suppose you do have to search for your materials. A textbook in the field of the paper will have some bibliographical information. The short bibliographies at the ends of some reference book entries are useful lists of the authorities on their subjects up to the time the reference books were compiled. The instructor in any one of your courses can tell you of books with bibliographies in his field. And there are many bibliographies especially designed to aid in particular subjects and fields. If you do not know the one you need, your reference librarian can point it out to you.

Let us take for an example Clarence Gohdes' *Bibliographical Guide to the Study of the Literature of the U.S.A.* (Durham, N. C., 1963). Since the word "literature" is broadly taken, the scope of the book is wider than the title may suggest. Suppose that you are interested in the American painter George Luks (1867–1933); you have seen some of his work in art galleries and reproductions, and you remember from an art appreciation course that he was one of "The Eight" and a member of the "Ash Can School." You think of discussing his work in its relationship to its time. You will not find Luks's name in any of the indexes to Gohdes' *Guide,* but either the subject index entry "painting" or the table of contents will lead you to the section heading "19. Arts Other Than Literature," and the sub-heading "Painting and Drawing." Under that sub-heading you will find these entries:

19.11   Richardson, Edgar P. *Painting in America: the story of 450 years,* N.Y., [1956]
        The appended selective bibliography makes a special point of museum exhibi-
   tion catalogs, which often contain reproductions of pictures.

19.15   Brown, Milton W. *American Painting from the Armory Show to the Depression.*
        Princeton, N.J., 1955.
        A history, chiefly of the realists, from the Ash Can School to the new realism,
   illustrated by T. H. Benton.

Now you have two usable secondary sources that will lead you to other sources.

Annotated bibliographies such as Gohdes' *Guide* are helpful; the bibliographical essays in some scholarly books, in which the authors discuss their own sources, may be even more helpful. And even if a scholarly book has no bibliography, its documentation will lead into its sources. But no book or bibliography can be quite up to date on the most recent publication, and you had better use the card catalog to see what your library may have in very recent books in the field of your paper.

Such a search as has been suggested, however, may result in an embarrassment of riches. When you have found, say, two promising sources, you had better stop and see where they lead you. You will find that your problem is not so much to find sources as it is to discriminate among sources. You may decide not to use at all some material you have found, or at one point to accept one source and not another. Indeed, a chief purpose of the source paper assignment is just that students may confront the problem of making such judgments. Of course they cannot be made on the basis of a subject index in a card catalog. But if you will examine, say, three books on the same subject and with somewhat parallel intentions, you may be surprised how easily you decide that for your purposes one is better than the others. Such a judgment may not be a judgment of quality—only a judgment about the book's usefulness to you. But of course it may also be a judgment of quality, for there are books not useful to any purpose. In a really stubborn problem in the discrimination of sources, seek your instructor's help.

You will need to discriminate among articles in periodicals in much the same way. But there you will begin by deciding what periodicals to use. Your own good sense will tell you not to consider articles in some magazines as source material, since you know that the quality of your paper will depend in good part on the quality of your sources. You may not use periodicals at all except for topics so recent that there is yet no treatment or no adequate treatment in books; then articles in periodicals will be principal sources.

The most generally useful index to magazines is the *Readers' Guide to Periodical Literature,* an author and subject index to many periodicals of general interest, issued twice a month except once a month in July and August, and collected in big yearly volumes, so that it is always nearly up to date. Some magazines have their own yearly indexes (e.g., *Scientific American*) and there are numerous special subject indexes and bibliographies of periodical articles. The only index to newspapers is the *New York Times Index;* since newspapers print the same news of national interest pretty much on the same day, it serves as an index to daily papers all over the United States.

The Use of Reference Books

Some reference books may be useful and legitimate secondary sources. For example, the *Dictionary of National Biography* (for Britons) or the *Dictionary of American Biography* may be the most convenient source of biographical information on prominent figures, and the only sources for less well-known persons. In a paper on Mark Twain's *Life on the Mississippi,* for instance, a student might use the entry in the *DAB* on Horace Bixby, the pilot under whom Twain served his apprenticeship. Although the entry in the *DAB* is largely based upon Twain's book, it gives some information that Twain does not: that Bixby's dates are 1826–1912, that during the Civil War he was chief of the Union River Service, and that after the war he was captain of the famous *City of Baton Rouge*. In many papers which are only incidentally concerned with biographical material, the *DNB* or the *DAB* may have the status of a secondary source.

Of course you will often use reference books for separate items of information, even though the books are not technically sources for your paper. Many students seem to turn to the multivolume encyclopedias when they might much better use specialized, compact reference books. For instance, Richard B. Morris' *Encyclopedia of American History* is easy to use, and often supplies a bit of information more precisely than bigger works will. Some of the entries in the one-volume *Columbia Encyclopedia*—those on scientific matters, for example—are clearer if less extensive than the parallel entries in the multivolume works, and the entries on place names are excellent. You can often quickly turn up a bit of information in *Brewer's Dictionary of Phrase and Fable* that may take a half-hour to find elsewhere—if you find it at all. The *Oxford Companion to American Literature*, and the similar Oxford companions to English, French, and Classical literatures, to music, and to the theatre are all useful and easy to use. *The World Almanac and Book of Facts* for the current year is often the most readily available source for recent statistical information. *Who's Who in America* offers biographical information about living Americans, and there are comparable works for other nations. Finally, your own desk dictionary may be a greater resource than you think; it is easy to overlook the resource nearest at hand.

Bibliography Cards and Bibliography

Once you have determined to use a particular source, you will need to make a card with adequate bibliographical information about it. Bibliographical information is adequate when it unmistakably identifies a book or an article in a periodical, with sufficient information to allow a reader to find it in a library. Eventually this information will be necessary for your preparation of footnotes (Chapter 5) and perhaps for a full bibliography.

Books. For most books the necessary information is this:
— the author's name (last name first, for alphabetizing)
— the title (underlined, the sign of italics)
— the place of publication
— the publisher's name
— the date of publication.
But for some books, one or more of these items may be necessary:
— the name of the editor
— the name of the translator
— the number of volumes, if there are more than one
— the number of any edition other than the first.

You will always take this information from the title page and—often for
the date of publication—the copyright page. In books published in this country, the last copyright date is ordinarily the date of publication. If you cannot
determine the date of publication, use the abbreviation n.d. (no space after
first period) in place of the date. In paperback reprints, be careful to distinguish between the copyright date of the original book and the date of the
reprint; it is the latter you will use in the bibliography card and later in footnotes to identify your reprint. (Of course the date of first publication may
often be significant for your purpose, and frequently you will need to use
it in the text of your paper.) Since there may be several paperback reprints
of well-known works, bibliographical entries for paperbacks (and later footnotes) may require the names of publishers' series: Laurel Editions, American
Century Series, and the like. Be sure your bibliography cards are accurate—
it will save you time and trouble in the end.

Here are some sample bibliography cards. They illustrate the kinds of entries
with which you are most likely to be concerned. Notice the order in which the
information is presented in each example. Notice also the punctuation, abbreviations, and spacing.

1. Most of your entries will be as simple as this first one.

> McDermott, John Francis. The Lost Panoramas of the
> Mississippi. Chicago: University of Chicago
> Press, 1958.

2. Addition of name of state to place of publication to prevent confusion
(in this instance with Cambridge, England).

> Hunter, Louis C. Steamboats on the Western Rivers:
> An Economic and Technological History. Cambridge,
> Mass.: Harvard University Press, 1949.

3. A volume in a series. The entry in this example indicates that Taylor's
book is the fourth volume in the series called *The Economic History of the
United States*.

> Taylor, George Rogers. The Transportation Revo-
> lution 1815-1860, The Economic History of the
> United States IV. New York: Rinehart & Company,
> Inc., 1951.

4. A work in more than one volume, with a translator.

> Tocqueville, Alexis de. <u>Democracy</u> <u>in</u> <u>America,</u>
> trans. Henry Reeve. 2 vols. New York: George
> Adlard, 1838.

5. A work in two volumes, with an editor. (Some persons would begin the following entry thus: Twain, Mark [Samuel L. Clemens]; the bracketed insertion is unnecessary with a well-known pseudonym like this, but such identification is desirable with one less well known.)

> Twain, Mark. <u>Mark</u> <u>Twain's</u> <u>Letters,</u> ed. Albert Bige-
> low Paine. 2 vols. New York: Harper & Brothers,
> 1917.

6. A work with two authors and no date.

> Gothland, Algernon B. and Cecil K. Cockloft. <u>Metri-</u>
> <u>cal</u> <u>Studies.</u> Baltimore: Banal and Prim, n.d.

7. An anthology, with two editors, in its second edition.

> Lowry, Howard Foster and Willard Thorp, eds. <u>An</u>
> <u>Oxford</u> <u>Anthology</u> <u>of</u> <u>English</u> <u>Poetry</u>. 2d ed. New
> York: Oxford University Press, 1956.

8. A single essay from a work with many authors. Notice that the title of the essay is in quotation marks, that when both volume and page numbers appear no abbreviations are used, and that when there are more than three editors (as here) one may use the name of the first listed and the abbreviation "et al." (But "and others" may also be used.)

> Wecter, Dixon. "Literary Culture on the Frontier,"
> <u>Literary</u> <u>History</u> <u>of</u> <u>the</u> <u>United</u> <u>States</u>, ed. Robert
> E. Spiller et al., II, 652–662. New York: The
> Macmillan Company, 1948.

Periodicals. Bibliographical form for articles in periodicals differs from that for books only as the conditions of publication differ. In the sample card below, notice that the title of the article is in quotation marks, that the underlined title of the periodical is followed by the volume number, the month and year in parentheses, and the page numbers (inclusive) on which the article appears. Notice the punctuation.

```
Todd, C. Lafayette. "Some Nineteenth Century Euro-
   pean Travellers in New York State," New York His-
   tory, 43 (October 1962), 336-370.
```

The form for a weekly publication is a little different. Notice that, since no volume number is used, the abbreviation for "pages" is used with the page numbers.

```
Iglauer, Edith. "A Reporter at Large: A Place to
   Live," The New Yorker, September 24, 1966, pp.
   188-220.
```

Your bibliography cards are primarily a record of your sources and the basis for the documentation of the paper. Where there is a library call number for the source, you might pencil it on the bibliography card, too.

Papers written with the documentation in which you are instructed in Chapter 5 do not necessarily have a listing of the bibliography at the end. If your instructor wishes you to append a bibliography to your paper, you have the sample forms here. That bibliography will be simply an alphabetized list of your bibliography cards, typed the full length of the line you use in your paper, with the run-over lines indented at the left margin as they are on the cards. Head it with just the word "Bibliography," and double space between entries. In alphabetizing, put "Mac" and "Mc" before "M." If you have an entry without an author's name, it is alphabetized by title, with the initial article, if any, ignored in the alphabetizing. Thus an entry for "The Mississippi Sternwheelers" would appear just that way, but would be alphabetized under "M."

Some of the conventions of form and documentation in the research paper may be new to you. Although at first they may seem inordinately complex, they are merely means to clarity and precision. Do not try to memorize forms; rather keep following the examples until their usages become habitual with you. In order to facilitate that practice, this book has an index designed to enable you to find quickly examples or discussion of any specific forms or details of style that you are likely to need. As you work on your paper, keep using the index to check any matter until you are in no doubt about it. The first entry in the index (under "abbreviations") explains all the abbreviations you are likely to use or to encounter.

2 how sources are used

In a source paper, the materials from the sources are woven together in a new pattern that is the writer's own. Before examining the kinds of patterns that may be achieved, you will have to consider the ways in which single passages from sources can be used. You will use your materials in two main ways. Sometimes you may quote directly. More often you will reduce the material by restatement. But in practice the matter is a bit more complex than that, and some distinctions are needed. This chapter will consider two techniques of quotation and three of restatement, and then illustrate each one.

Quotation. When a substantial passage is of special importance to a paper, and there is good reason not to handle it in restatement, it may be quoted in full. But you had better not do that very often, for papers with a preponderance of long quotations are immediately suspect—what looks at first sight like padding usually proves to be exactly that. It is generally better to quote briefly; but how frequently you quote you will decide according to your material and purpose.

Short quotations are run into the text of the paper, in quotation marks of course. Quotations that will make more than five or six lines of your text are single spaced and separated from the text by triple spacing. Such quotations may also be indented from each margin. Quotation marks are not used around them, since the single spacing is a sign of quotation. In the quotation of verse, any passage of more than two lines is quoted as verse (single spaced and centered); a single line of verse is run into the text in quotation marks; and two lines may be run into the text if they are separated by the mark called a slash or virgule: "And yonder all before us lie / Deserts of vast eternity." Quotations of any kind must be accurate, just as they appear in the sources. The one permissible change is a change in the capitalization of a quoted bit of prose, in order to fit it into the source paper writer's own sentence.

If you need to insert anything in a quotation, do so in square brackets, which will indicate that the insertion is not part of the quoted writer's text. A reference for a pronoun may be inserted in this way: "He [Mr. Brown] would be 'so full of laugh' that he could hardly begin." Or sometimes an inserted expla-

11

nation is convenient: "From St. Joe [St. Joseph, Missouri] to Sacramento . . . ." If your typewriter does not have brackets, type parentheses and make them into brackets with your pen. If there is a mistake in the quoted passage do not correct it. You may indicate your awareness of the mistake by insert-ing the Latin word for "thus" after it in this way: "The new law had no great affect [sic] on the worst offenders." But be sure you do not put "sic" after some permissible or archaic form and reveal your own unawareness.

Quotation is something of an art; but the art depends primarily upon intel-ligent reading. If you can quote the heart of a chapter or a page, you have a real control of your material. Quotations in papers on literary subjects, in which there is a concern with the writer's style or technique, may offer spe-cial problems, some of which will be illustrated later.

Quotation with Ellipsis. A passage that is too long to quote entire may often be handled by omitting a part or parts. Any omission within a quotation is indicated by three . . . *spaced* periods, called ellipsis points. Suppose you have these three sentences from George Lyman Kittredge's introduction to *Hamlet:* "Hamlet cannot act upon mere spectral evidence. The testimony of the Ghost must somehow be corroborated. The murderer must be forced to testify against himself." You could quote the passage omitting the second sentence: "Hamlet cannot act upon mere spectral evidence. . . . The mur-derer must be forced to testify against himself." The ellipsis points show that there is an omission; the other period is of course the period required for end punctuation. When a paragraph or more is omitted from a quotation (or a line or more from a verse quotation), the omission is indicated by a line of spaced periods the length of the lines of the quoted material. But in student papers the occasion for such omission will be rare.

Some passages are easy to excise; some cannot be handled by excision. You will have to determine, according to your purpose, whether or not the matter you think of omitting can be spared. Of course you must not change or pervert the writer's meaning.

Summary Restatement. When you restate from a source, remember that you are restating. Summary restatement does not mean just changing a few words here and omitting bits there; nor does it mean paraphrasing. You will of course "put the passage into your own words," but you will do so in a way that effects a considerable reduction. Without that considerable reduction, the restate-ment is usually unjustified — you might as well quote. The principle is this: quote, or restate and reduce.

Summary Restatement Including Brief Quotation. Restatement may, and often should, include brief quotation; you will find this technique frequently useful and convenient when the wording of particular source phrases is im-portant. At first you may need to take special care that your own summary account and the quoted bits are grammatically consistent: for example, your source may be written in its writer's present, and you, since you are writing an account of past events, may be writing in the past tense, so that you will need to handle your quotations so as to avoid tense inconsistency.

Interpretive Accounts. Occasionally you may have to handle a passage by making your account of it also an interpretation. The occasion will be when, for the purposes of your paper, it is important that your reader know just how you mean him to understand the passage, or when you mean to focus his attention on some particular quality of the passage. Such an account will not necessarily be shorter than the passage, since you are including interpretive discussion within your account.

At this point the demonstration will start over, and show how all five ways of using a source passage can be illustrated by five handlings of one passage. Of course you will understand that all five ways would not be equally good in any one paper; in each illustration there is a somewhat different kind of interest and purpose. The passage used for illustration is a part of Mark Twain's account of the education of an apprentice pilot.

From Mark Twain, *Life on the Mississippi.* New York: Harper & Brothers, 1950.

77 The face of the water, in time, became a wonderful book — a book that was a dead language to the uneducated passenger, but which told its mind to me without reserve, delivering its most cherished secrets as clearly as if it uttered them with a voice. And it was not a book to be read once and thrown aside, for it had a new story to tell every day. Throughout the long twelve hundred miles there was never a page that was void of interest, never one that you could leave unread without loss, never one that you would want to skip, thinking you could find higher enjoyment in some other thing. There never was so wonderful a book written by man; never one whose interest was so absorbing, so unflagging, so sparklingly renewed
78 with / every re-perusal. The passenger who could not read it was charmed with a peculiar sort of faint dimple on its surface (on the rare occasions when he did not overlook it altogether); but to the pilot that was an *italicized* passage; indeed, it was more than that, it was a legend of the largest capitals, with a string of shouting exclamation points at the end of it, for it meant that a wreck or a rock was buried there that could tear the life out of the strongest vessel that ever floated.

Notice in the reprinting above that the page numbers from the book used as source are printed in the margin. When consecutive pages are reprinted and the end of a page does not coincide with the end of a paragraph, the point at which one page ends and another begins is indicated by a slash mark, thus /. In all subsequent reprinting of sources, the same indications of pagination will be included, so that the documentation of the passages written from the sources may be illustrated.

Quotation

One purpose that would justify an extended quotation from the foregoing source passage is the illustration of Twain's style, and that purpose will be here exemplified. Of course the writer will have to provide some context for the quotation; a quotation should not just be thrown at the reader in the hope that he will make something of it. Assume that this paragraph is part of a discussion of Twain as stylist, and so closely related to what has gone before that it needs no connecting first sentence.

Twain often carefully calculates his effects. A striking instance is the elaborate extended metaphor in his account of the
education of the apprentice pilot. "The face of the water," he says,
"became a wonderful book," a book that one had to learn to read:

> There never was so wonderful a book written by man; never one
> whose interest was so absorbing, so unflagging, so sparklingly
> renewed with every re-perusal. The passenger who could not
> read it was charmed with a peculiar sort of faint dimple on
> its surface (on the rare occasions when he did not overlook it
> altogether); but to the pilot that was an _italicized_ passage;
> indeed, it was more than that, it was a legend of the largest
> capitals, with a string of shouting exclamation points at the
> end of it, for it meant that a wreck or a rock was buried there
> that could tear the life out of the strongest vessel that ever
> floated. (pp. 77-78)

The quotation is single spaced. The first line of the quotation is not indented; nor would it be even if it were the beginning of a paragraph. If, however, two or more paragraphs were quoted consecutively (which would happen but rarely), the first line of each would be indented. The page citation in paren-theses follows the quotation immediately. It might have been made in a foot-note, but this is a simpler way. Since this page citation identifies a quotation separated by single spacing from the text of the paper, the citation follows the period of the quotation. For this sort of parenthetical page citation, the source used must have been clearly identified at the first reference to it. This kind of documentation will be discussed in Chapter 5.

Something, too, may be said about the sentences that introduce the quota-tion. The source should always be clear from the text itself. The assumption here is that the title _Life on the Mississippi_ has been used in the foregoing para-graphs, and that it will be clear that the writer is continuing to use the book. The expression "he says" is used because one thinks of a book existing in the present: one says "the Bible says," or "Shakespeare says." The last sentence of the writer's preparation for the quotation ends with a colon because it for-mally introduces the quotation. But a colon is not to be used in such a way that it breaks up a grammatical structure. If, for instance, the expression "Twain describes the river as" were used to introduce some quotation, there would be no punctuation after it.

Quotation with Ellipses

In the following illustrative paragraph, the writer is in the midst of a review of Twain's account of the cub pilot's education. But he wishes his reader to realize, too, something of the quality of Twain's style, although he is not concerned with it technically, as was the writer of the paragraph just considered. The first sentence of the paragraph is transitional.

> The apprentice pilot, then, had to learn the shape of the river. He had to learn, too, what the appearance of the water could tell him. Twain writes with a certain excitement about this part of the pilot's education:

>> The face of the water, in time, became a wonderful book. . . . Throughout the long twelve hundred miles there was never a page . . . that you would want to skip. . . . The passenger who could not read it was charmed with a peculiar sort of faint dimple on its surface . . . ; but to the pilot that was an <u>itali-</u><u>cized</u> passage; . . . for it meant that a wreck or a rock was buried there that could tear the life out of the strongest vessel that ever floated. (pp. 77–78)

The passage happens to be easy to excise, and the example has rather more ellipses than are common — the better, perhaps, for exemplary purposes. The best way for you to understand the technique is to make a careful comparison with the full text of the original, and to note in each instance how the ellipsis points have been used. The procedure is easy to state: the three spaced periods indicate omission; the other marks of punctuation are used according to ordinary principles of punctuation and as Twain uses them.

Ellipsis points may also be used at the end of a substantial quotation (whether separated from the text or run in) when it is desirable to indicate that the passage has been broken off before completion — that one is not quoting all the writer had to say on the matter. Ellipsis points may likewise be used at the beginning of a substantial quotation if that quotation does not begin at the beginning of a sentence. This usage is illustrated on page 27.

Summary Restatement

The relative fullness of the restatement depends upon the importance of the passage for the writer's purpose. In the example below, assume a paper on the apprentice pilot's education; there is not so much reduction, therefore, as there might be in another context. The first sentence is transitional.

> The apprentice pilot, then, had to learn the shape of the river. He also had to learn, Twain tells us, the significance of the ever-changing appearance of the surface of the water. To the initiates, the surface of the water was like a book that told a fascinating, ever-new story throughout twelve hundred miles of river. And the information the surface of the water gave the pilot was often vital. According to Twain, a kind of faint dimple on the water, that a passenger might admire if he noticed at all, would alert the pilot to a submerged wreck or rock, one that could destroy a steamboat (pp. 77–78).

In a summary restatement, you need not write a formal précis, and you may make your purpose in using the passage emerge, so long as you do not pervert its meaning. Notice that here, although the passage is restated, the terms used in the passage are not always avoided. For example, there would be no good substitute for "faint dimple," no other term that one could be sure would convey Twain's meaning. Notice, too, the citation of the page numbers of the original passage; it is just as necessary to indicate the source for a summary account as it is for a quotation. Since the parenthetical page citation is here part of the text, it appears *before* the final period.

In a different source paper about Twain or about river piloting, one in which the account of learning the face of the water has less importance than it does in a study of the river pilot's education, a summary account might be as brief as this:

> The apprentice pilot had to learn not only the shape of the river, but also the meaning of certain signs on the surface of the water. For instance, one sign, a faint dimple, might tell him where there was a submerged wreck or rock (pp. 77–78).

Summary Restatement Including Brief Quotation

A restatement will often include certain phrases quoted from the source and carefully worked into the summary. The effect of this example may not be greatly different from that of the example above; certainly it conveys the same information. Perhaps you may feel that the quotations help draw attention to Twain's metaphors.

> The apprentice pilot, then, had to learn the shape of the river. He also had to learn, Twain tells us, to read "the face of the water," to read it as "a wonderful book," an ever-changing story of twelve hundred miles of river, with "never a page . . . that you would want to skip." The uninstructed passenger might be "charmed with a peculiar sort of faint dimple on its surface," but the pilot who could read the face of the water, found that dimple "an <u>italicized</u> passage," warning of a submerged "wreck or a rock . . . that could tear the life out of the strongest vessel that ever floated" (pp. 77–78).

Notice that the ellipsis points need be used only to show omissions within quotations. You need *not* write ". . . charmed with a peculiar sort of faint dimple on its surface . . ." — as a good many students evidently have been taught. The practice may not be wrong, but it is unnecessary, for it is perfectly clear that such quotations are not complete. Notice, too, the convention for citation at the end of quotations with quotation marks. In such instances, the parenthetical reference comes after the quotation mark but before the period, or before the comma if the reference does not come at the end of a sentence. But exclamation points and question marks do not change their position when there is a parenthetical reference.

Interpretive Account

The next example is intended to show how an interpretive account can focus attention on a special quality in the source. Assume that the example is part of a source paper concerned with the way in which Twain's character emerges in his early writing. The first sentence is transitional, with the first clause looking back at what has just been discussed, and the second clause leading forward.

Twain's account of learning the shape of the river shows how much he enjoyed his initiation into the mysteries of piloting, and he writes with as much gusto of a second stage in his education as a pilot, his learning to know "the face of the water." It became for him a fascinating, ever-changing book: "There never was so wonderful a book written by man; never one whose interest was so absorbing, so unflagging, so sparklingly renewed with every re-perusal." And he seems to have delighted in the way in which a pilot's knowledge set him apart from the rest of mankind, so that what for the uninstructed passenger was only "a faint dimple" on the surface of the water was for the pilot a warning of a submerged wreck or rock that might destroy a steamboat (pp. 77–78). But this gusto is a quality of <u>Life</u> <u>on</u> <u>the</u> <u>Mississippi</u> from the beginning. Twain's delight in praising what he enjoyed is the chief charm of his early work, for through that praise his readers recover the enjoyment.

Here, at the end of these five examples, is one comment that applies to them all. Even though one assumes purposes for which the passage is important, these treatments of it are quite long enough. It is not easy at first to write with enough economy to give your paper substance and use a reasonably large body of source material. You will probably find that you do not get this economy in first draft writing; it is likely you will have to manage it, at least to begin with, in careful revision.

The Use of Secondary Sources

Secondary sources *are* secondary, and they will have a secondary part in your paper. Ordinarily you will not quote at any length from them, and you will be more likely to use particular pieces of information from them (properly acknowledged) than to restate passages from them. A secondary source that might be used in a paper concerned with *Life on the Mississippi* is Louis C. Hunter's *Steamboats on the Western Rivers* (Cambridge, Mass., 1949). Consider here how it might be useful.

When one reads Hunter's section on piloting (pp. 240–259), he sees that Hunter accepts Twain's account with little reservation, and that he is using Twain as a source. You will recognize that this sentence is clearly drawn from Twain: "'He [the pilot] must be able to read the color and texture of the water's surface for indications of what lay beneath; he must be familiar with all the clues to the presence of hidden obstructions." It would be rather silly to quote this sentence or one like it when you were dealing with Hunter's source for it. But here is another passage:

> The literature of steamboating, by dwelling on the spectacular and making capital of the layman's naïveté, has elevated matters of normal professional skill to the level of the miraculous. Mark Twain's classic picture of steamboat piloting, we must remember, was colored by a reminiscent and nostalgic mood as well as by a professional interest in telling a good story well.

If you were writing on *Life on the Mississippi,* Hunter's expert judgment would have at least an interest for you. And if you were concerned with the quality of Twain's record, you might use, or even quote, the first sentence; the matter of the second sentence would probably have emerged in your discussion.

Often a secondary source will be useful in broadening your own background. For instance, in his account of sounding (Chapter XII), Twain speaks of a boat being hung up on a reef, and remarks, "Then she has to while away several hours (or days) sparring herself off." Twain says no more of "sparring," but you can find a detailed account in Hunter (pp. 254–255). Or suppose you were dealing with Twain's account of the *Pennsylvania* disaster (Chapter XX), and you wished to show that it was a typical steamboat explosion. You might draw the beginning of a paragraph from Hunter (pp. 541–542).

The <u>Pennsylvania</u> explosion, according to Louis C. Hunter, was one of three major disasters on the lower Mississippi in 1858 and 1859, and on the western rivers entire there were fifty explosions during the years 1848–1852.[3] Twain's account of the <u>Pennsylvania</u> explosion . . .

Citation of a secondary source is ordinarily made by a footnote; notice the number for the footnote in the passage above.

Combining Sources in a Short Paper: An Example

Thus far the chapter has shown some ways of handling sources. The next step is to consider how sources may be combined. And one must consider, too, how their combination is controlled by the purpose of the paper — how the pattern of the paper is attained. The following illustration shows how a student might go about writing a paper that uses only a few pages of source material.

The student works with a set of three related selections such as might be part of his reading in courses in history, political science, history of public education, sociology, or American literature. There are two by Thomas Jefferson and one by John Adams. The assumption is that the student has them all in a book of readings used as a textbook in a course he is taking, that they are part of regularly assigned material, and that the student has been assigned a paper on the concepts of "natural aristocracy" in Jefferson and in Adams.

This student has no problem, then, in finding his material for this course paper, and its concentration has been virtually determined for him. His principal problem will be to determine the pattern of his paper. Now this student, for example, might be a little ahead of you: he has had some experience in this sort of writing. Perhaps you can gain something by watching him work.

The student will know from his instructor's remarks when he assigned the selections that John Adams and Thomas Jefferson were contemporaries, political opponents, and, at least in the latter portion of their lives, good friends who discussed in an interesting series of letters their opinions on political and other matters. He will know, too, that Jefferson's *Notes on the State of Virginia* is a book of general information about Virginia, written much earlier than the letters and in answer to a set of queries from the Secretary of the French Legation in Philadelphia—which explains the curious section designation Query XIV. Here are the selections. You will need to read them with some care in order to see how the student uses them.

From Thomas Jefferson's Letter to John Adams of October 28, 1813, as reprinted in *Writer to Reader,* ed. Neal Frank Doubleday. Boston: D. C. Heath and Company, 1966.

367 . . . I agree with you that there is a natural aristocracy among men. The grounds of this are virtue and talents. Formerly, bodily powers gave place among the aristoi. But since the invention of gunpowder has armed the weak as well as the strong with missile death, bodily strength, like beauty, good humor, politeness and other accomplishments, has become but an auxiliary ground for distinction. There is also an artificial aristocracy, founded on wealth and birth, without either virtue or talents; for with these it would belong to the first class. The natural aristocracy I consider as the most precious gift of nature, for the instruction, the trusts, and government of society. And indeed, it would have been inconsistent in creation to have formed man for the social state, and not to have provided virtue and wisdom enough to manage the concerns of the society. May we not even say, that that form of government is the best, which provides the most effectually for a pure selection of these natural aristoi into the offices of government? The artificial aristocracy is a mischievous ingredient in government, and provision should be made to prevent its ascendancy. On the question, what is the best provision, you and I differ; but we differ as rational friends, using the free exercise of our reason, and mutually indulging its errors. You think it best to put the pseudo-aristoi into a separate chamber of legislation, where they may be hindered from doing mischief
368 by their co-ordi- / nate branches, and where, also, they may be a protection to wealth against the agrarian and plundering enterprises of the majority of the people. I think that to give them power in order to prevent them from doing mischief is arming them for it, and increasing instead of remedying the evil. For if the co-ordinate branches can arrest their action, so may they that of the co-ordinates. Mischief may be done negatively as well as positively. Of this, a cabal in the Senate of the United States has furnished many proofs. Nor do I believe them necessary to protect the wealthy; because enough of these will find their way into every branch of the legislature to protect themselves. From fifteen to twenty legislatures of our own, in action for thirty years past, have proved that no fears of an equalization of property are to be apprehended from them. I think the best remedy is exactly that provided by all our constitutions, to leave to the citizens the free elec-

tion and separation of the aristoi from the pseudo-aristoi, of the wheat from the chaff. In general they will elect the really good and wise. In some instances, wealth may corrupt, and birth blind them; but not in sufficient degree to endanger the society.

It is probable that our difference of opinion may, in some measure, be produced by a difference of character in those among whom we live. From what I have seen of Massachusetts and Connecticut myself, and still more from what I have heard, and the character given of the former by yourself, who know them so much better, there seems to be in those States a traditionary reverence for certain families, which has rendered the offices of the government nearly hereditary in those families. I presume that from an early period of your history, members of those families happening to possess virtue and talents have honestly exercised them for the good of the people, and by their services have endeared their names to them. In coupling Connecticut with you, I mean it politically only, not morally. For having made the Bible the common law of their land, they seem to have modeled their morality on the story of Jacob and Laban.[1] But although this hereditary succession to office with you may, in some degree, be founded in real family merit, yet in a much higher degree it has proceeded from your strict alliance of Church and State.[2] These families are canonised in the eyes of the people on common principles, 'you tickle me, and I will tickle you.' In Virginia we have nothing of this. Our clergy, before the revolution, having been secured against rivalship by fixed salaries, did not give themselves the trouble of acquiring influence over the people. Of wealth, there were great accumulations in particular families, handed down from generation to generation, under the English law of entails. But the only object of ambition for the wealthy was a seat in the King's Council. All their court was paid to the crown and its creatures; and they Philipised[3] in all collisions between the King and the people. / Hence they were unpopular; and that unpopularity continues attached to their names. A Randolph, a Carter, or a Burwell must have great personal superiority over a common competitor to be elected by the people even at this day. At the first session of our legislature after the Declaration of Independence, we passed a law abolishing entails. And this was followed by one abolishing the privilege of primogeniture, and dividing the lands of intestates equally among all their children, or other representatives. These laws, drawn by myself, laid the axe to the root of pseudo-aristocracy. And had another which I prepared been adopted by the legislature, our work would have been complete. It was a bill for the more general diffusion of learning. This proposed to divide every county into wards of five or six miles square, like your townships; to establish in each ward a free school for reading, writing and common arithmetic; to provide for the annual selection of the best subjects from these schools, who might receive, at the public expense, a higher degree of education at a district school; and from these district schools to select a certain number of the most promising subjects, to be completed at an University, where all the most useful sciences should be taught. Worth and genius

[369 marginal note]

[1]Laban, Jacob's father-in-law, exploited Jacob, but Jacob at length outwitted him (Genesis 29–31). Jefferson is saying that the people of Connecticut have patterned their morality on an Old Testament story in which neither of the main characters seems very admirable.

[2]Jefferson refers to a hold-over of the close relationship between church and state in Massachusetts and Connecticut established at their founding as colonies.

[3]An allusion to Athenian history. Jefferson means that in all disputes between the British government and the Virginia colony, the wealthy supported the British government. Randolph, Carter, and Burwell are example names of old and wealthy Virginia families.

would thus have been sought out from every condition of life, and completely prepared by education for defeating the competition of wealth and birth for public trusts. My proposition had, for a further object, to impart to these wards those portions of self-government for which they are best qualified, by confiding to them the care of their poor, their roads, police, elections, the nomination of jurors, administration of justice in small cases, elementary exercises of militia; in short to have made them little republics, with a warden at the head of each, for all those concerns which, being under their eye, they would better manage than the larger republics of the county or State. A general call of ward meetings by their wardens on the same day through the State would at any time produce the genuine sense of the people on any required point, and would enable the State to act in mass, as your people have so often done, and with so much effect, by their town meetings. The law for religious freedom,[4] which made a part of this system, having put down the aristocracy of the clergy, and restored to the citizen the freedom of the mind, and those of entails and descents nurturing an equality of condition among them, this on education would have raised the mass of the people to the high ground of moral respectability necessary to their own safety, and to orderly government; and would have completed the great object of qualifying them to select the veritable aristoi, for the trusts of government, to the exclusion of the pseudalists; and the same Theognis who has furnished the epigraphs of your two letters, assures us that ["Good men, Cyrnus, have never ruined a state"]. Although this law has not yet been acted on but in a small and inefficient degree, it is still considered as before the legislature, with other bills of the revised code, not yet taken up, and I have great hope that some patriotic spirit will, at a favorable moment, call it up, and make it the key-stone of the arch of our government.

With respect to aristocracy, we should further consider, that before the estab-lishment of the American States, nothing was known to history but the man / of
370 the old world, crowded within limits either small or overcharged, and steeped in the vices which that situation generates. A government adapted to such men would be one thing; but a very different one, that for the man of these States. Here every one may have land to labor for himself, if he chooses; or, preferring the exercise of any other industry, may exact for it such compensation as not only to afford a comfortable subsistence, but wherewith to provide for a cessation from labor in old age. Every one, by his property, or by his satisfactory situation, is interested in the support of law and order. And such men may safely and advantageously reserve to themselves a wholesome control over their public affairs, and a degree of freedom, which, in the hands of the *canaille* of the cities of Europe, would be instantly perverted to the demolition and destruction of everything public and private. The history of the last twenty-five years of France, and of the last forty years in America, nay of its last two hundred years, proves the truth of both parts of this observation.

But even in Europe a change has sensibly taken place in the mind of man. Science has liberated the ideas of those who read and reflect, and the American example has kindled feelings of right in the people. An insurrection has conse-quently begun, of science, talents, and courage, against rank and birth, which have fallen into contempt. It has failed in its first effort, because the mobs of the cities, the instrument used for its accomplishment, debased by ignorance, poverty, and

[4] In colonial Virginia the Anglican Church was the established church, supported by all tax-payers. Jefferson refers to a law abolishing this relationship.

vice, could not be restrained to rational action. But the world will recover from the panic of this first catastrophe. Science is progressive, and talents and enterprise on the alert. Resort may be had to the people of the country, a more governable power from their principles and subordination; and rank, and birth, and tinsel-aristocracy will finally shrink into insignificance, even there.[5] This, however, we have no right to meddle with. It suffices for us, if the moral and physical condition of our own citizens qualifies them to select the able and good for the direction of their government, with a recurrence of elections at such short periods as will enable them to displace an unfaithful servant, before the mischief he meditates may be irremediable.

I have thus stated my opinion on a point on which we differ, not with a view to controversy, for we are both too old to change opinions which are the result of a long life of inquiry and reflection; but on the suggestions of a former letter of yours, that we ought not to die before we have explained ourselves to each other. We acted in perfect harmony, through a long and perilous contest for our liberty and independence. A Constitution has been acquired, which, though neither of us thinks perfect, yet both consider as competent to render our fellow citizens the happiest and the securest on whom the sun has ever shone. If we do not think exactly alike as to its imperfections, it matters little to our country, which, after devoting to it long lives of disinterested labor, we have delivered over to our successors in life, who will be able to take care of it and of themselves.

From John Adams' Letter to Thomas Jefferson of November 15, 1813, as reprinted in *Writer to Reader.*

371   We are now explicitly agreed upon one important point, viz., that there is a natural aristocracy among men, the grounds of which are virtue and talents. You very justly indulge a little merriment upon this solemn subject of aristocracy. I often laugh at it too, for there is nothing in this world more ridiculous than the management of it by all the nations of the earth; but while we smile, mankind have reason to say to us, as the frogs said to boys, what is sport to you are wounds and death to us. When I consider the weakness, the folly, the pride, the vanity, the selfishness, the artifice, the low craft and mean cunning, the want of principle, the avarice, the unbounded ambition, the unfeeling cruelty of a majority of those (in all nations) who are allowed an aristocratical influence, and, on the other hand, the stupidity with which the more numerous multitude not only become their dupes, but even love to be taken in by their tricks, I feel a stronger disposition to weep at their destiny, than to laugh at their folly. But though we have agreed in one point, in words, it is not yet certain that we are perfectly agreed in sense. Fashion has introduced an indeterminate use of the word talents. Education, wealth, strength, beauty, stature, birth, marriage, graceful attitudes and motions, gait, air, complexion, physiognomy, are talents, as well as genius, science, and learning. Any one of these talents that in fact commands or influences two votes in society gives to the man who possesses it the character of an aristocrat, in my sense of the word. Pick up the first hundred men you meet, and make a

[5]Jefferson is, of course, referring to the French Revolution. He is saying that, although the Revolution seemed to end in futile violence and excess, the general change in thinking of which it was a part will inevitably move forward and ultimately succeed.

republic. Every man will have an equal vote; but when deliberations and discussions are opened, it will be found that twenty-five, by their talents, virtues being equal, will be able to carry fifty votes. Every one of these twenty-five is an aristocrat in my sense of the word, whether he obtains his one vote in addition to his own by his birth, fortune, figure, eloquence, science, learning, craft, cunning, or even his character for good fellowship, and a *bon vivant*. . . .

Your distinction between natural and artificial aristocracy does not appear to me founded. Birth and wealth are conferred upon some men as imperiously by nature as genius, strength, or beauty. The heir to honors, and riches, and power, has often no more merit in procuring these advantages than he has in obtaining a handsome face or an elegant figure. When aristocracies are established by human laws, and honor, wealth, and power are made hereditary by municipal laws and political institutions, then I acknowledge artificial aristocracy to commence; but this never commences till corruption in elections become dominant and uncontrollable. But this artificial aristocracy can never last. The everlasting envies, jealousies, rivalries, and quarrels among them; their cruel rapacity upon the poor ignorant people, their followers, compel them to set up Caesar, a demagogue, to be a monarch, a master; *pour mettre chacun à sa place*.[1] Here you have the origin
372 of all artificial / aristocracy, which is the origin of all monarchies. And both artificial aristocracy and monarchy, and civil, military, political, and hierarchical despotism have all grown out of the natural aristocracy of virtues and talents. We, to be sure, are far remote from this. Many hundred years must roll away before we shall be corrupted. Our pure, virtuous, public-spirited, federative republic will last forever, govern the globe, and introduce the perfection of man; his perfectibility being already proved by Price, Priestley, Condorcet, Rousseau, Diderot, and Godwin.[2] Mischief has been done by the Senate of the United States. I have known and felt more of this mischief than Washington, Jefferson, and Madison, all together. But this has been all caused by the constitutional power of the Senate, in executive business, which ought to be immediately, totally, and essentially abolished. Your distinction between the [aristoi] and [pseudo-aristoi] will not help the matter. I would trust one as well as the other with unlimited power. The law wisely refuses an oath as a witness in his own case, to the saint as well as the sinner. . . .

You suppose a difference of opinion between you and me on the subject of aristocracy. I can find none. I dislike and detest hereditary honors, offices, emoluments, established by law. So do you. I am for excluding legal, hereditary distinctions from the United States as long as possible. So are you. I only say that mankind have not yet discovered any remedy against irresistible corruption in elections to offices of great power and profit, but making them hereditary.

From Thomas Jefferson, *Notes on the State of Virginia* (1784), as reprinted in *Writer to Reader*.

[1]The French expression means "to put everyone in his place."
[2]In the three sentences beginning "We, to be sure . . ." and ending with the list of names, Adams is writing with a heavy sarcasm. The three English thinkers (Price, Priestley, and Godwin) and the three French thinkers (Condorcet, Rousseau, and Diderot) were part of the movement of mind that Jefferson refers to in IV of our selection from his letter to Adams. Adams probably believes Jefferson too close to their opinions. The belief in perfectibility typically arose from the conviction that man was not by nature bad, and that by the use of his reason he would ultimately make a good society. The six thinkers are not, however, so nearly identical in their views as the passage implies.

372 QUERY XIV. *The . . . description of the laws?*

Another object of the revisal[1] is to diffuse knowledge more generally through the mass of the people. This bill proposes to lay off every county into small districts of five or six miles square, called hundreds, and in each of them to establish a school for teaching reading, writing, and arithmetic; the tutor to be supported by the hundred, and every person in it entitled to send their children three years gratis, 373 and as much longer as they please, paying for it; these schools to be under a / visitor who is annually to choose the boy of best genius in the school, of those whose parents are too poor to give them further education, and to send him forward to one of the grammar schools, of which twenty are proposed to be erected in different parts of the country, for teaching Greek, Latin, geography, and the higher branches of numerical arithmetic. Of the boys thus sent in any one year, trial is to be made at the grammar schools one or two years, and the best genius of the whole selected, and continued six years, and the residue dismissed. By this means twenty of the best geniuses will be raked from the rubbish annually, and be instructed, at the public expense, so far as the grammar schools go. At the end of six years' instruction, one half are to be discontinued (from among whom the grammar schools will probably be supplied with future masters); and the other half, who are to be chosen for the superiority of their parts and disposition, are to be sent and continued three years in the study of such sciences as they shall choose, at William and Mary College, the plan of which is proposed to be enlarged, as will be hereafter explained, and extended to all the useful sciences. The ultimate result of the whole scheme of education would be the teaching all the children of the state reading, writing, and common arithmetic; turning out ten annually, of superior genius, well taught in Greek, Latin, geography, and the higher branches of arithmetic; turning out ten others annually, of still superior parts, who to those branches of learning shall have added such of the sciences as their genius shall have led them to; the furnishing to the wealthier part of the people convenient schools at which their children may be educated at their own expense. The general objects of this law are to provide an education adapted to the years, to the capacity, and the condition of everyone, and directed to their freedom and happiness. . . . By that part of our plan which prescribes the selection of the youths of genius from among the classes of the poor, we hope to avail the state of those talents which nature has sown as liberally among the poor as the rich, but which perish without use, if not sought for and cultivated. But of all the views of this law none is more important, none more legitimate, than that of rendering the people the safe, as they are the ultimate, guardians of their own liberty. For this purpose the reading in the first stage, where *they* will receive their whole education, is proposed, as has been said, to be chiefly historical. History, by apprising them of the past, will enable them to judge of the future; it will avail them of the experience of other times and other nations; it will qualify them as judges of the actions and designs of men; it will enable them to know ambition under every disguise it may assume; and, knowing it, to defeat its views. In every government on earth is some trace of human weakness, some germ of corruption and degeneracy, which cunning will

---

[1]"The revisal" is a proposed revisal of Virginia law. Jefferson's *Notes on the State of Virginia* is a collection of information about Virginia written in answer to questions from the secretary of the French legation in Philadelphia, and first published in France. Jefferson wrote the book in 1781–2, more than thirty years before his letter to Adams. You have seen that in 1813 he had by no means given up his plan.

discover, and wickedness insensibly open, cultivate, and improve. Every government degenerates when trusted to the rulers of the people alone. The people themselves therefore are its only safe depositories. And, to render even them safe, their minds must be improved to a certain degree. This indeed is not all that is necessary, though it be essentially necessary. An amendment of our constitution must here come in aid of the public education. The influence over government must be shared among all the people. If every individual which composes their mass participates of the ultimate authority, the government will be safe; because the corrupting the whole mass will exceed any private resources of wealth; and public 374 ones cannot be provided but by levies on the people. In this case every / man would have to pay his own price. The government of Great Britain has been corrupted, because but one man in ten has a right to vote for members of Parliament. The sellers of the government, therefore, get nine tenths of their price clear. It has been thought that corruption is restrained by confining the right of suffrage to a few of the wealthier of the people; but it would be more effectually restrained by an extension of that right to such members as would bid defiance to the means of corruption.

Lastly, it is proposed, by a bill in this revisal, to begin a public library and gallery, by laying out a certain sum annually in books, paintings, and statues.

The Student at Work on His Paper. The student chooses "Adams and Jefferson on Natural Aristocracy" as the title for his paper, thinking it as definitive a title as he can get within a reasonable length. He is familiar with the sources he is to use and he has them at hand; he can therefore work directly from them, without note cards. His problem will be the reworking of his source materials into a new fabric designed to accomplish a defined and strictly limited purpose.

The beginning of his paper, our student knows, ought to make the scope and purpose of the paper entirely clear. And he has had enough experience to realize that a short paper will not carry an introduction, that he needs to get to the matter in hand at once. Realizing that he may have to revise later, he writes this paragraph as a point of departure:

Late in their lives, long after their active careers were over, John Adams and Thomas Jefferson discussed in a series of letters not only former days but their present convictions. In a particularly interesting pair of letters, each defines his concept of "natural aristocracy." Although they share the term, the difference in the way in which they intend it points up an important difference in their thinking. It is the purpose of this paper to distinguish the two definitions.

This book will consider later the whole problem of getting source papers off the ground. The point to notice here is that the student is willing to commit himself to his purpose, to make a sort of contract with his readers in simple, straightforward terms.

Now observe the student at some crucial points in his paper: the first when he has come to the place in which he must define Jefferson's concept of "natural aristocracy." He decides, rightly, that at this point he should quote Jefferson directly; but he realizes that he must weave the quotation skillfully into the fabric of the paper. And a little consideration shows him that his readers will need a distinction between "natural aristocracy" and "aristocracy" in the ordinary sense. He sees how he can make the distinction a starting point for the definition:

What is ordinarily called "aristocracy"—that group of persons powerful and distinguished by social position or inherited wealth—Jefferson, in his letter to Adams of October 28, 1813, calls "pseudo-aristocracy." But Jefferson does recognize another kind of superiority—one that might be politically and socially useful. He insists that "there is a natural aristocracy among men. The grounds of this are virtue and talents. . . . The natural aristocracy I consider as the most precious gift of nature, for the instruction, the trusts, and government of society." The status of a person as a natural aristocrat, then, has nothing to do with his means or social position, for it depends upon inherent excellence and ability. In his <u>Notes on the State of Virginia</u>, Query XIV, Jefferson speaks of "those talents which nature has sown as liberally among the poor as the rich."

The student must of course also make clear what Adams means by "natural aristocracy." He sees that he must let his reader know that, for Adams, modifying "aristocracy" by "natural" does not really change the sense of the noun. After some reflection he writes:

When Adams uses the term "natural aristocracy" he intends us to understand that aristocracies are inevitable. As he sees it, all aristocracies are "natural" in their origin, for they begin when gifted persons take power and position, as they will always do. In his letter to Jefferson of November 15, 1813, he makes his idea clear in an account of a hypothetical republic:

Pick up the first hundred men you meet, and make a republic. Every man will have an equal vote; but when deliberations and discussions are opened, it will be found that twenty-five, by their talents, virtues being equal, will be able to carry fifty votes. Every one of these twenty-five is an aristocrat in my sense of the word, whether he obtains his one vote in addition to his own by his birth, fortune, figure, eloquence, science, learning, craft, cunning, or even his character for good fellowship. . . .

Adams therefore says to Jefferson: "Your distinction between natural and artificial aristocracy does not appear to me to be founded." He is saying that men become aristocrats by their talents, to be sure, but that there are many talents besides those of the intellect.

Our student feels that he is learning how to put materials together and that he is getting along pretty well. Toward the end of his paper, however, he comes to a problem that gives him a good deal of trouble before he solves it. He has established Jefferson's concept of natural aristocracy; he has made clear the difference between the thought of Adams and Jefferson on the whole matter or aristocracy. It is now time to write an account of Jefferson's Virginia plan for education, to explain for his readers how Jefferson intended to discover natural aristocrats and to assure the state of their services.

Now at once our student sees that he has a choice. Jefferson's description of the plan in his letter to Adams (beginning "It was a bill . . .") is short enough to quote entire. His more extended account in *Notes on Virginia* would have to be handled in summary. Our student feels that it would surely be well to have the account in Jefferson's own words, and so he thinks at first that he will use the passage from Jefferson's letter. But he remembers that an important matter is not covered in the passage from the letter: that passage does not make at all clear the rigor of the selection Jefferson intends. Perhaps, he thinks, the better way would be to write a formal summary of the passage from *Notes on Virginia*. Yet he is reluctant to relinquish the quotation.

Then it occurs to him that perhaps he can use the quotation as a center for the discussion and extend it by reference to the *Notes on Virginia* passage. Such combination of sources is difficult, even for more experienced writers than our student; but after two or three false starts he finds the way he wants to do it. His final version is this:

An essential feature of Jefferson's plan was a system for rigorous selection of those students who should be educated at the state's expense and for its service. In his letter to Adams he describes the system in a general way. He proposes

. . . to divide every county into wards of five or six miles square . . . ; to establish in each ward a free school for reading, writing and common arithmetic; to provide for the annual selection of the best subjects from these schools, who might receive, at the public expense, a higher degree of education at a district school; and from these district schools to select a certain number of the most promising subjects, to be completed at an University.

In Query XIV of his Notes on the State of Virginia, Jefferson is much more specific. The free education provided by the wards is to be a three-year education (although a child may continue longer if his parents will pay). The "annual selection" from the ward schools is to be the selection in each of the best boy student among those from families of small means. These students are to be sent to one of the twenty district grammar schools that Jefferson hopes to have established. In the grammar schools these brilliant boys will have a trial year or two. Then, in each grammar school, the one best boy student among them will be selected to finish grammar school (six years in all). At the end of grammar school, these twenty will be

divided in half: the ten "to be completed at an University" will go
to William and Mary College at state expense; the other ten will end
their formal education (and, Jefferson thinks, may well become
grammar school teachers). At three times in the system, then, there
will be a rather ruthless elimination; the survivors will be supposed to have demonstrated their status as "natural aristocrats."

What pleases the student about his final version is the close connection he
has managed between the quoted passage and the development of it based
on *Notes on the State of Virginia*. He got that connection by picking up bits
of the quoted passage in his development, and by keeping the development
parallel to the quoted passage.

It is unnecessary here to follow the student further in his labors—you will
have been able to see how he is going at them. You would do well to go back
to the sources to find the passages the student uses, and to consider the relationship of the paper to its sources. Of course you have been watching the
student at the most difficult points in his paper, when he was weaving in quotations, always a problem for the unpracticed writer. You could easily finish
the paper for him; it might run 1500 words when complete.

The student has not included footnotes or page citations; his instructor did
not require that sort of documentation for this short paper, and indeed there
would have been little point in citing the page numbers of a textbook, since
he could not assume all readers could easily get to it. Yet the paper is documented; it does inform the reader about the sources in the text; and the reader,
with no great trouble, could find the sources in standard editions of Jefferson
and Adams.

3 the use of note cards

In the example of combining sources in the last chapter, the student was working directly from a small body of source material reprinted in a textbook. This chapter will consider note taking and the combination of source materials that have been reduced to a set of note cards. Two principles must be firmly established at the outset.

One is that the writer of the source paper should take his notes with the purpose of his paper clearly in mind. He should not even begin until he has some familiarity with his major sources and knows what he is taking notes for. Otherwise he will take a great many notes useless to his paper. The source paper writer cannot take notes efficiently until he can foresee a possible use for each note he takes. He will need to decide, even as he takes his notes, when he may wish to quote a passage, and to get that passage accurately recorded and in quotation marks. He will need to decide when he can record the substance of a passage in the briefest restatement.

The second principle is this: Each note must deal with a single matter. The whole purpose of taking notes on note cards is defeated unless this principle is adhered to, for the convenience of note cards is that they may be arranged and rearranged in the order they are to be used. Indeed, some writers find that they can do some of the organization of their papers by trial arrangements of their cards.

Of course you will recognize that these principles will be applied in one way when you work on a book that you can keep on your desk while you are writing the paper, and in another way when you are working in the library on sources that you will not have before you as you write. When you are dealing with a book that you can return to at any time, you can take such brief notes as will lead you back to the text. It might be sensible, for example, not to copy out a passage you think of using as a quotation, but merely to indicate to yourself its subject matter and that it is quotable. But the notes you take in the library must be intelligible some time after they have been taken, the quotations must be accurate, and the distinction between quotation and restatement must be unmistakable—so that when you write the paper you will know what you have and what you are doing.

The Purpose of the Notetaking and the Sources

In this example, assume that the notetaking is done in the library, and that the paper is to be written without the sources for the notes at hand. The topic of the paper is slavery in the United States in the second quarter of the nineteenth century as it was described by certain foreign observers. It is a good topic, because foreign observers traveling in America could take a more detached view of the "peculiar institution" of slavery than Americans themselves could. Here are the sources.

From Alexis de Tocqueville, *Democracy in America,* trans. Henry Reeve. 2 vols. New York: George Adlard, 1838.

I,   When I contemplate the condition of the South, I can only discover two al-
359 ternatives which may be adopted by the white inhabitants of those States; viz.
either to emancipate the Negroes and to intermingle with them, or, remaining
isolated from them, to keep them in slavery as long as possible. All intermediate
measures seem to me likely to terminate, and that shortly, in the most horrible of
civil wars and perhaps in the extirpation of one or the other of the two races. Such
is the view which the Americans of the South take of the question, and they act
consistently with it. As they are determined not to mingle with the Negroes, they
refuse to emancipate them.
  Not that inhabitants of the South regard slavery as necessary to the wealth of
the planter; for on this point many of them agree with their Northern countrymen
in freely admitting that slavery is prejudicial to their interests; but they are convinced that, they hold their lives upon no other tenure. The instruction which is
now diffused in the South has convinced the inhabitants that slavery is injurious
to the slave-owner, but it has also shown them, more clearly than before, that it
is almost an impossibility to get rid of its bad consequences. Hence arises a singular
contrast; the more the utility of slavery is contested, the more firmly is it established in the laws; and while its principle is gradually abolished in the North, that
selfsame principle gives rise to more and more rigorous consequences in the South.

I,   Whatever may be the efforts of the Americans of the South to maintain slavery,
361 they will not always succeed. Slavery, which is now confined to a single tract of
the civilized earth, attacked by Christianity as unjust and by political economy as
prejudicial, and which is now contrasted with democratic liberties and the intel-
ligence of our age, cannot survive. By the choice of the master, or by the will of
the slave, it will cease; and in either case great calamities may be expected to
ensue. If liberty be refused to the Negroes of the South, they will in the end forcibly
seize it for themselves; if it be given, they will abuse it ere long. . . .

From Charles Augustus Murray, *Travels in North America.* 2 vols. London: Richard Bentley, 1839.

I, The abject submission and ignorance *necessary* to the continuance of slavery
166 may be easily gathered from the following statement: — The farms of two gentlemen whom I visited occupied the whole of a peninsula formed by the James River:
they had each two overseers; thus (their families being young) the effective strength

of white men on their estates amounted to *six:* the negroes were in number about
two hundred and fifty: nor was there a village or place within many miles from
which assistance could be summoned. Let the reader only imagine the scene that
must have ensued had some of these blacks, while smarting under the pain of the
lash, been taught the first crude notions of natural right, or been awakened to the
first consciousness of their power, or been excited to one feeling of indignation or
revenge strong enough to overcome the habitual terror of the cowhide! Hence it
is not difficult to understand how justly the slave-holders urge the necessity of
keeping from their slaves all glimpses of knowledge or liberty upon the ground of
self-preservation; and thus the best apology for slavery furnishes the best evidence
of its inhuman unholy nature.

But to return to the plantations on James River. There is a wide difference be-
I, tween the respective conditions of the domestic and the farm-labouring slave; the
167 former has, in many instances, been / brought up under the same roof with his
owner — perhaps they have been playmates in early boyhood; he has rarely, if ever,
felt the lash; and his respectability of demeanour and attachment to the family are
characteristics which it is easy and pleasant to observe; his punishment when idle
is generally confined to scolding, and if that fails, a threat to sell him will almost
always reduce the most obstinate to obedience. But the farm-labouring slave is
little brought into contact with his master, whose habitual feelings of humanity are,
therefore, seldom excited in his favour: he is one of a gang from which, as from a
team of horses, a certain quantum of labour is expected; he is entirely at the mercy
of the overseer; and the merit of that functionary in the eyes of his employer being
to extract the maximum of profit from the exertions of the slaves, he is apt to spare
neither threats nor blows in the discharge of his office, and an appeal against him
to the master is worse than hopeless, as the negro evidence is unheeded: The com-
plainant, therefore, is well aware that by accusing his oppressor, he would only
draw upon himself redoubled severity or cruelty. These overseers are generally
men of harsh and unfeeling character, which every day spent in their disagreeable
vocation must have a natural tendency to harden; but I have never heard in the
I, Southeastern States of their being guilty of the licentious atrocities of which they
168 have been / sometimes accused in Louisiana, and which certainly are but too common among them in the West India Islands.

The Note Cards

Of course the first thing the notetaker does with either source is to make a
bibliography card for it, following the form illustrated in Chapter 1. Having
that card, he will make only the briefest indications of the source on his note
cards, for he will use the bibliography card for the rest of the information necessary in documentation. He gives each note card a subject heading at the upper
left and an indication of source and page number or numbers at the upper
right. The subject heading is a catch word or phrase that identifies the subject
of the note, a fairly specific word or phrase, but not so specific that it does not
allow several cards with the same subject heading. Occasionally the notetaker
will write, below the body of the note, a sort of note to himself, suggesting a
significance or possible comparison.

In the example notes below, the notetaker has taken notes more frequently
than is usual, for almost all of the material in the passages is close to the pur-

pose of his paper. When he has predicted a possible quotation in his paper, he has included the quotation in his notes.

South caught in trap   Tocqueville
                                                  I, 359

T. sees only two possibilities for South: "to emancipate the Negroes and to intermingle with them, or
. . . to keep them in slavery as long as possible."
Anything in between likely to end in war between
races. "As they are determined not to mingle with
the Negroes, they refuse to emancipate them."

South caught in trap   Tocqueville
                                                  I, 359

Southerners did not think slavery an advantage to
them, but neither did they believe it possible to get
rid of it.
   (See Dickens, American Notes, pp. 291-293)

South caught in trap   Tocqueville
                                                  I, 361

T. says religious and social sentiment against slavery so strong that it could not survive. But what he
seems to have expected was a revolt of the Negroes:
"By the choice of the master, or by the will of the
slave, it will cease; . . . . If liberty be refused
to the Negroes of South, they will in the end forcibly
seize it for themselves."

South caught in trap   Murray
                                                  I, 166

Example of why Southerners kept slaves in "abject
submission": M. visited two farms which made up whole
of peninsula in James River (Va). 1 owner and 2 overseers for each farm: six able-bodied white males and
250 Negroes in this isolated place. Suppose what
would happen if slaves incited to revolt. ". . . thus
the best apology for slavery furnishes the best evidence of its inhuman unholy nature."

```
What slavery was like                    Murray
   domestic and farm                     I, 166-167

Wide difference between domestic and farm laboring
slave. Domestic slave often / brought up with owner,
usually treated kindly, often had affection for
owner's family. Farm laboring slave had little con-
tact with owner and at mercy of overseer whose job it
was to get all work possible out of slaves. Overseers
usually men of unfeeling nature, hardened by their
employment.
```

This last card illustrates a precaution in notetaking. Notice the slash mark: it indicates exactly what appears on each of the two pages of the original. Although the notetaker has considered Murray's comparison of the domestic and farm laboring slave one matter and expects to use it so, it might turn out that, in his paper, he discusses the farm laboring slave separately and therefore uses only the last part of the note in that discussion. If so, he will know which page to cite. This precaution — so easy to take — saves trouble in the writing of the paper.

Notes into Paper

The process of working notes into your paper cannot be fully shown by example in this book. A source paper writer must think about all his notes together, and that evaluation could not be illustrated in any reasonable space. In this case it is evident that the last note on the Murray passage, though doubtless useful in some separate discussion of the overseer, or of domestic and farm laboring slaves, does not relate well to the other material. But the passage from Tocqueville and page 166 of the Murray passage have a close relationship, for Murray furnishes concrete illustration for Tocqueville's generalized assertion. The writer might experiment to see how the notes on these passages of source material could be combined. In order that the examples be complete, they will be documented, even though the instruction in documentation does not come until Chapter 5.

If the Tocqueville passage is to be used in the paper as a central statement of the slaveholders' dilemma, the combination of notes might be in this fashion:

```
The fear of a revolt on the part of slaves was ever-present in the
second quarter of the nineteenth century. Alexis de Tocqueville
apparently did not foresee the Civil War that did come about; he
foresaw a civil war between slaves and slaveholders. He points
out that the slaveholders, caught in the institution they had made,
had but two choices: "to emancipate the Negroes and to intermingle
with them, or . . . to keep them in slavery as long as possible."
And he decides that since the slaveholders "are determined not to
```

mingle with the Negroes, they refuse to emancipate them." Even so, Tocqueville says, the institution of slavery could not be permament: "By the choice of the master, or by the will of the slave, it will cease. . . . If liberty be refused to the Negroes of the South, they will in the end forcibly seize it for themselves."[5]

The danger Tocqueville envisions was thought very real by another European observer, Charles Augustus Murray. He describes two farms which made up the whole of the James River peninsula in Virginia, and which were therefore isolated. On these farms there were six able-bodied white males and 250 Negroes. Suppose, Murray says, what must happen if the slaves were to be incited to revolt. In fear of such revolt, he says, the slaveholders understandably held the slaves in the most "abject submission"; and he remarks that "thus the best apology for slavery furnishes the best evidence of its inhuman unholy nature."[6]

[5]Democracy in America, trans. Henry Reeve (New York, 1838), I, 359 and 361.
[6]Travels in North America (London, 1839), I, 166.

(Notes in this form would be used for the paper's first reference to these writers.)

Here is another possibility. In the following example, assume that the Tocqueville passage would be used in combination with parallel discussions by other foreign observers of the slaveholders' dilemma. The threat of black rebellion would still need discussion, and the Tocqueville-Murray notes might be combined in this way:

The belief that a revolt of Negro slaves was possible and even probably is apparent in the work of these foreign observers. Tocqueville, indeed, seems to have expected that the end of slavery would come about through a slave revolt, and Murray describes for us an example of the conditions that made for a fear of black rebellion. He visited two farms isolated together on a peninsula in the James River in Virginia. On these two farms there were 250 Negroes and only six able-bodied white males. Murray asks his readers to imagine what would have happened had a revolt started, and suggests that it is really no wonder that slaveholders kept the slaves in "abject submission."[11]

[11]Tocqueville, I, 361; Murray, I, 166.

(The form of this note assumes the writers have been previously cited in the paper.)

You might do well now to go back and compare the note cards and the source passages, and then the note cards and the example passages from the assumed paper. In the latter comparison, notice the tenses — some students have a little difficulty with tense in term paper writing.

4 planning the structure

When should the structure of your paper be planned? It cannot be, of course, until you have done a good deal of your reading, and until you have a control of your sources and know your purpose. But if you can pretty well settle the problem before you are far into your notetaking, notetaking will be more selective and therefore more efficient. Do not long delay, then, your encounter with the problem of structure. The most practiced writer continually finds that some segment of his best planning does not work, that he must try another way. The student source paper writer who does not allow himself time enough for trial and error is in trouble.

Planning begins with analysis. The analytic process should not be new to you; in all your writing you have been concerned with the division of subjects for orderly discussion. Your experience has taught you that this division cannot be arbitrary. You have considered your reader on the one hand and your subject on the other, and you have tried to separate the parts of your subject so that they will be distinct for orderly discussion, and yet be understood in their relationships to each other. What is new in source paper writing is that the material may be somewhat less tractable than the material of your own experience and observation. Your sources are what they are. What may seem in the abstract a sensible or even an eminently logical division is no good if your sources give you little or no material for one of the planned sections. In planning a source paper you will need to consider your readers, your topic and purpose with it, and the materials your sources furnish you.

Chronological Analysis

In some papers the divisions may be time divisions. If the topic is a consecutive series of events or the development of a set of ideas, the division is a separation into stages. A writer needs the method of chronological analysis whenever an ordinary narrative treatment is not economical enough for his purpose, or when it will not make clear the relationship of the parts of development one to another.

This sort of separation into stages is often entirely obvious. Ronald E. Shaw's *Erie Water West: A History of the Erie Canal 1792–1854* (1966) has for its first three sections: "The Prophecy" (from first suggestions to enabling act), "The Grand Canal" (period of construction), and "On Erie Water" (first period of operation). One could hardly imagine this material separated in any other way. Of course no student paper would have such a sweep as this book; but a student writing on the legend and folklore of the Erie Canal might well separate his paper into sections defined by the period of construction and the period of early operation. Or, for another example of an inherent time division, suppose a discussion of the development of pendulum clocks. Christian Huygens' application of the principle of the pendulum to clockwork would almost surely define one stage; the invention of the anchor escapement would as surely define another.

But time divisions may not be so obviously inherent in the subject. Suppose a student intends to write an ambitious paper to be called "The NAACP and the Supreme Court." His stages might conceivably be the tenures of the executive directors of the Association, so that the tenure of Walter White might distinguish one stage, and that of Roy Wilkins another. But without taking a hard look at his source material, the student could not be sure; perhaps the decisions of the Supreme Court would better mark off the sections of the paper. The 1954 decision that segregation in public schools is unconstitutional might then mark the beginning of the last stage, or perhaps the next-to-last stage, in the paper.

Then there is another consideration. A good time division for one concentration in a subject may not serve for another concentration in the same subject. Suppose a student in a course in marketing is writing a paper on the development of air conditioning. He might distinguish these three periods: a period when air conditioning was largely designed for theatres and restaurants (just a little later for stores and public buildings), a period when it extended to room air conditioners for homes and offices, and a period when home owners began to exchange room air conditioners for central air conditioning. Perhaps for his purpose these three stages would work well; but they would hardly serve another student interested in the engineering of air conditioners, even though the two students were using some of the same sources.

For some subjects, the method of chronological analysis does not require that every period of a time span be discussed. Suppose a student is working on a paper on Nathaniel Hawthorne's *American Notebooks*. A study of the whole would not be feasible; but when the student had surveyed his material and decided what seemed most interesting and representative, he might fix upon, say, the notebooks accounts of Hawthorne's six-week stay at North Adams, Massachusetts, in 1838; of his residence at Brook Farm in 1841; and of the first four months of his residence at the Old Manse after his marriage in 1842. And if a student writer finds that even the most economical treatment of a topic he has considered handling by chronological analysis makes too long a paper, his consideration may still be useful to him, for it is quite possible that he can write on but one of the stages he has distinguished. Of course your topic may not be one in which you can use the method of chronological analysis, but you can see that it is frequently a useful structure.

Division

When the topic is not a development and therefore cannot be handled in time stages, the parts of the topic yet have to be separated for orderly discussion. Such separation can simply be called division. Now when you are writing of natural objects or organisms, or of the material works of man, you find division no problem. If you were to write of a rifle, you would almost certainly organize your discussion by the parts it presents to your inspection: lock, stock, and barrel. But with papers that deal with ideas, the separation of parts has to be discerned in a careful consideration of the topic and the writer's purpose with it. The pattern of discussion does inhere in topic and purpose, but it usually is not merely to be observed, but rather to be discovered. Unless the pattern is discovered and established initially, the paper is likely to have no structure. A writer may have to revise his initial decision as he proceeds, but he will not have a pattern of discussion unless he plans one.

In order to illustrate the problem of division, assume some paper topics and consider the problems they offer. Suppose one has in hand a paper on Cincinnati, Ohio as it is described by three foreign observers in the second quarter of the nineteenth century. (Cincinnati was interesting to foreigners and Americans alike as a city thriving where there had been only wilderness a half-century before.) Now such a paper might be divided with a section for each of three observers. But that plan might well lead to repetitiousness or to disproportion—the most obvious way might not be the best way. A plan that provided separate discussion of the economic life, the social life, and the cultural life of the new city would probably work better. (There is an example passage in Chapter 7 that would fit into such a paper so divided.)

Now consider a somewhat similar problem with quite different material. A student in a course in marketing is writing a paper on the ways in which selling appeals are made to housewives in such household magazines as *American Home* or *Better Homes and Gardens*. He might, if he were using four magazines as his specimens, discuss each separately. But that would be uneconomical and probably repetitious. He could discover a better division by a consideration of his material. He might well have three sections: a first on the advertisements; a second on the articles; and a third on the way in which articles and advertisements are correlated in their appeal to the housewife anxious for the prestige of new possessions. (An example passage in Chapter 6 would fit into a paper so divided.)

Divisions for Literary Studies. A literary paper may offer problems a bit more difficult, since its divisions may also show a critical selection of the material. Suppose you are doing a paper on Mark Twain's *Adventures of Huckleberry Finn*, and that your special interest in the novel is the narrative point of view and the advantages of the use of Huck as both narrator and central character. You can hardly deal with all of Huck's experience. But you might separate out his realization of the frontier aristocrats, the Grangerfords; of the riverside confidence men, the Duke and Dauphin; and of Jim.

Another kind of paper, dealing with Hawthorne's *American Notebooks*, might be concerned with the relationships between the notebooks and Hawthorne's fiction. You could not organize this paper as a piece of chronological analysis, but you could find a selective division. The sections of the paper might be separate considerations (a) of the many brief suggestions for stories; (b) of the passages written as literary exercises; and (c) of the passages that were ultimately taken up into Hawthorne's fiction, particularly those used in "Ethan Brand" and in *The Blithedale Romance*. In this scheme you can see the necessity not only of a selective division but of a calculated order of discussion; here the second (b) matter must be discussed before the third, since some of what was written as pure exercise did eventually become a part of the fiction.

Thus far this chapter has been assuming fairly long papers. Now sometimes students who recognize the structural problem in a long paper seem to feel that a short paper will take care of itself. But the structure of a short paper may need as much care as that of a long one, although the problem presents itself somewhat differently. Suppose you are going to write a short paper concerned with John Wesley Powell and his importance in the history of conservation, a topic mentioned in Chapter 1. Now if you think — since you have an abundance of material and a short paper to write — that the material will simply fall into its own pattern of structure, you will be in great danger of writing a paper that could be honestly titled only "Some Unconnected Remarks about John Wesley Powell." But if you recognize the nature of the material and watch for its structural problems, you will find that the most important decision you have to make is to fix upon which of Powell's achievements, or which segment of his career, or what special knowledge or ability of Powell's will make the best discussion by itself. You will be making a sort of division at the outset of the whole subject, and separating out a part that you can purposively discuss, and that will have an integrity as it stands alone. To be sure, there will be a division in the paper itself, but it may be nothing more than paragraphing.

Outlines

A wise student will make at least a rough outline of a source paper before he attempts to write it. If a formal outline — topic or sentence — works for you, you certainly should have one. An outline does make the source paper writer conscious of structure, and it may reveal weaknesses in a planned structure before they are written into the paper. For this reason, some instructors like to see a formal outline well before the paper is due.

There are reasons, however, for scepticism about source paper outlines as they are often handled. In hundreds of classrooms, thousands of students have been required to submit formal outlines with their source papers. Experienced instructors know that very often these outlines were written last, even after the papers were typed and ready to hand in. They were no good to anyone, except as — possibly — some students, discovering that their papers could not be outlined, might have corrected some structural fault.

An outline is a means to an end — and should be so used. Some students, having learned a proper sequence for roman numerals, capital letters, arabic numbers, and small letters, have far too much confidence in the merely formal sequence, and allow it to conceal from them grave faults of logic in their plans. Or, for other students, the formal outline has too much finality; they stick with it even when it leads them into awkwardness in the actual handling of their material. But of course abuses of a technique do not invalidate it. Only be sure that if you make a formal outline, you make it work for you.

Two Special Provisions in Structural Plans

Most source papers will be organized overall either by chronological analysis or by division. We have yet to consider two problems of structure that frequently emerge in parts of papers. Your topic may not require you to face either; but in a good many topics a writer faces one or the other, or possibly both.

The Analysis of Problems. In the discussion of a problem, careful analysis is necessary in order to define its nature. Suppose you have found a concentration for that paper on John Wesley Powell. From Powell's several achievements you have separated out Powell's *A Report on the Lands of the Arid Region of the United States* (1878) for your discussion. Now in the first part of your paper you would need to analyze the problem that the report was intended to solve or to help solve. You would find the problem had such components as human greed, political advantages, American habits of mind, and traditional ways of dealing with lands in the public domain. And you would try to make clear to your reader how those components were interrelated in 1878, in order that the significance of Powell's report might be really clear to him.

No one can say before hand just how you should approach any particular problem you are to analyze—except to say that the method depends upon the nature of the problem. You will have to decide whether the problem needs statistical demonstration to show its extent, of a historical account of its development, or a definition of some previously unrecognized element or elements, or perhaps more than one of these. In the planning of your paper, there is no substitute for taking your problem apart to see what it is, so that you can deal with it for your reader.

The Discussion of Related Documents. Often students write papers concerned with the influence of one document upon another, with one document as a source for another, or with one document as a comment upon another. The third of these concerns is illustrated in the sample discussion of the Jefferson-Adams letters in Chapter 2; and Chapter 7, too, has example passages that would fit into papers concerned with the relationship of two works one to the other. The discussion of related documents requires a provision in the planning.

That provision is to make sure that the reader is clearly informed, before any comparative discussion is done, what the documents are, their dates, and the reason it is considered important to consider them together. The sample signpost paragraph for the Adams-Jefferson paper in Chapter 2 is intended to make a start in doing those things.

Now what has just been said in the paragraph above may seem too obvious to need saying. But it is deceptively easy to take for granted that what is in your mind is also in the reader's mind. You must keep remembering that your reader will not know what you intend unless you tell him. Moreover, if the nature of the documents and the purpose in dealing with them is made clear at the outset, the rather difficult procedures of discussing documents together can proceed without interruption.

This provision for the discussion of related documents will most often be required in papers not concerned with such relationship throughout. For example, the assumed paper about household magazines, and the assumed paper about the *American Notebooks* and Hawthorne's fiction would each in its last section present a fairly difficult problem of handling documents together. So also in many papers with literary or historical concerns, a portion or perhaps a whole section, will present this structural problem. But there will be some papers organized as discussions of related documents throughout.

As an example, consider one such paper. Suppose a student chooses to write about the relationship of Hamlin Garland's short stories and his autobiographical account of his early life. The student needs to begin with a description of the works in general terms and with a rather broad indication of the purpose of the subsequent discussion—one that he can sharpen as he goes on. The first paragraph of his paper will indicate what his preliminary planning has been:

Although Hamlin Garland wrote a great deal, only two of his books are now much remembered: <u>Main</u>-<u>Travelled</u> <u>Roads</u> (1891), short stories about the difficult lives of Midwestern farmers; and <u>A Son of the Middle Border</u> (1917), an autobiographical account of his boyhood and youth. Both books have the same background of experience, although in <u>A Son of the Middle Border</u> Garland is looking back on it in long perspective. A consideration of the two books together will help to define the connections of the short stories with Garland's early experience and observation.

The student's problems of structure are of course not solved in this paragraph, but it does suggest a method of working from the short stories to the autobiographical book. That would seem a convenient pattern, since discussions of the six stories one by one would make a division for the paper. That division would serve to keep the focus sharp and avoid the discussion of portions of *A Son of the Middle Border* not related to the short stories.

5 documentation

Source papers are not written so that they may be festooned with footnotes. What is needed is a documentation that is at once adequate, simple, clear, and consistent. "The conventions of documentation," the *MLA Style Sheet* says, "are largely means to an end, to enable the reader to follow up your sources with ease."

Problems that are sometimes overlabored in classrooms will disappear if the student keeps that end in mind. The purpose of documentation is not primarily the acknowledging of indebtedness—although of course it does do that. But the text of a source paper itself makes clear that the writer is working with sources, and in general what those sources are. The documentation allows the reader, if he wishes, to go back to the sources for himself, to see quotations in their context, to judge whether the sources have been understood and properly represented, and perhaps to follow a newly acquired interest of his own. Usually footnotes and page references within the text simply tell *where* the sources are to be found; the reader will consult them or not as his interests lead him.

Neither completeness nor clarity, therefore, should ever depend upon a footnote. And even in the identification of sources, the text of the paper ought to let the reader know what the major sources are. If you are dealing with only a few sources, you can certainly manage to name them all in the text of the paper.

It may be desirable to point out that information readily available in many places does not need documentation, even if it is also in a source one is using. One does not document an undisputed date, for instance, or the location of a city, or the fact that Napoleon was defeated at Waterloo, or the fact that the Sahara is an arid region. But if one were using statistics about the mean rainfall in the Sahara, he would of course show where he got them.

This chapter will consider the more important conventions of documentation. And in the next chapters many of the example passages will be documented, so that within this book you will have samples for all, or almost all, of the documentation with which you may be concerned. Now getting citation and footnote form right is merely a matter of following examples, which anyone can do. Your instructor will eventually lose patience with any student who cannot follow a model. If you do happen to encounter some out-of-the-way problem in footnoting for which this book furnishes no sample, *The MLA Style Sheet* probably will; if it does not your instructor can recommend a form.

The methods of documentation in which you are instructed in this chapter provide adequate bibliographical information, so that a paper documented according to this instruction requires no bibliography for the identification of sources.

Titles and Writers' Names

The conventions for handling titles in academic writing are simple. Underline (to indicate italics) the titles for published books, plays, pamphlets, long poems, and periodicals — in general any title that designates a separate publication. But there is an important exception: the title the Bible, the titles of the books thereof, and the titles of other sacred scriptures are not underlined. Put within quotation marks the titles of articles, short stories, poems, and chapters — in general what is part of a book or appears within a periodical. Although these conventions are not followed in newspapers and in some periodicals, they are always to be followed in academic writing. They make for clarity and economy. *"Hamlet* without Hamlet" clearly distinguishes the play from the character. If you refer to Robert Frost's "After Apple-Picking" and to his *North of Boston* in the same passage, your reader will know which is the title of a poem and which is the title of a volume.

The first time any writer of any source is mentioned in your text, use the name in full as it appears on the title page. In subsequent references, these are the conventions: With the last name of a living male writer, or of one recently deceased, use "Mr." (or "Dr." or "Professor" as appropriate). But do not use "Mr." with the name of a writer some time dead; in a paper on Matthew Arnold one would write: "When Arnold wrote 'Dover Beach' . . . ." But the titles "Miss" or "Mrs." should always be used with the last names of women.

Documentation Within the Text

Documentation may often be included within the text and without footnotes. Footnotes are to be avoided when they can be without an awkwardness disconcerting to the reader. As was evident in Chapter 2, once the information about a source that is extensively used has been given in a footnote, all subsequent page references to it may be made in parentheses within the text. But often it is feasible to make all references within the text. When you refer in your text to a work by author and title, it takes only a little more space to put in the place of publication, date, and page number. One way to do it is this: "Edmund Wilson in *Patriotic Gore* (N. Y., 1962, p. 231) points out that . . . ." And when you cite a standard reference work, always avoid a footnote: you may say, for example, "According to the *Oxford Companion to American Literature*, fourth edition, an actual John Henry may have lived."

No reader will have trouble identifying the work, and since it is alphabetized, a page number is neither necessary nor proper. Here is a paragraph in
which all the documentation is parenthetical:

The nineteenth-century American novels we value today were often
not very well known in their time. James D. Hart tells us that Nathaniel Hawthorne's The Blithedale Romance had a first printing
in 1852 of 5,090 copies and second printing of only 2,350 more, but
that Fanny Fern's Fern Leaves from Fanny's Portfolio sold 70,000
copies in the single year 1853 (The Popular Book, Berkeley, 1961,
pp. 92-93). No novel by William Dean Howells or by Henry James appears in Professor Hart's "Chronological Index" of books widely
read in their time, although Francis Marion Crawford and Archibald
Clavering Gunter, now almost forgotten, were vastly popular in
the late 1800s (pp. 187-189). Of the great American novelists of
the nineteenth century, only Mark Twain seems to have had really
wide sales in his time (pp. 146-150). But small sales did not entirely discourage good writers; perhaps it is necessary to have
many poor books that a few good ones may emerge. At any rate, as was
written long ago in Ecclesiastes, "of making many books there is
no end" (12:12).

References to all works that have line or verse numbering can be easily
worked into your text. The best form for Biblical citation is the use of arabic
numbers for book numbers and chapter and verses: Luke 16:13, 2 Kings
2:18–19. (In some cases, naming your Bible will help to avoid some confusions
among citation systems in different versions — notably with Douay and King
James.) Plays may be cited by act, scene, and line or lines in this fashion: *Measure for Measure,* III.i.72–79. Long poems may be cited by book or part and
line number or numbers: *Paradise Lost,* II, 629–642. If you or your instructor
prefer other recognized forms, they may be used, but do be sure you are consistent. For instance, use the same form for citation not only for one play, but
for all plays referred to in your paper.

Almost always it is best to handle references to the Bible, to plays, and to
long poems parenthetically. You will of course let your reader know what
edition of a play or of a long poem you are using. Here are two passages to
illustrate such parenthetical reference. Since they have been contrived for
illustrative purposes, reference is more frequent than would be at all likely
in a paper you might write. Each example includes the preparatory footnote
that establishes the source.

After The Murder of Gonzago has been interrupted, Hamlet's
doubts about the ghost are all resolved. He had said to Horatio that
if the king did not reveal his guilt, "It is a damned ghost that we
have seen" (III.ii.87).[1] The king does clearly reveal his guilt,
and Hamlet says exultingly, "O good Horatio, I'll take the ghost's
word for a thousand pound!" (III.ii.297-298) The doubt Hamlet had

expressed at the end of Act II was the doubt of a reasonable man, and we had been made aware of its basis early in the play, particularly by Horatio's warning (I.iv.69–78). But now the action of Claudius himself has proved the ghost the "honest ghost" (I.v.138) Hamlet had believed it to be in his excitement and awe at its first appearance to him.

[1]References to Hamlet in this paper are to the single volume edition of George Lyman Kittredge (Boston, 1939), which uses a standard line numbering.

"An Essay on Criticism" is interesting not only as a critical document; it is also an amusing poem. Pope has a happy way of parodying the poetic faults he condemns. These lines, for instance, represent verse that is only "correct" and regular:

> While expletives their feeble aid do join,
> And ten low words oft creep in one dull line.
>   (II, 146–147)[1]

And if Pope would censure the fashion of using a closing line of twelve syllables and six stresses, he writes a mocking one:

> A needless Alexandrine ends the song,
> That, like a wounded snake, drags its slow length along.
>   (II, 156–157)

Perhaps the couplet just quoted illustrates Pope's doctrine that "The sound must seem an echo to the sense" (II, 165) as well as the several couplets he offers to exemplify it—couplets which may themselves be a little mocking in their intent. This seems to be the most successful of them:

> When Ajax strives some rock's vast weight to throw,
> The line, too, labours, and the words move slow.
>   (II, 170–171)

The sort of thing Pope is doing in these couplet is perhaps a trick, but it requires skill and sure control.

[1]The text of An Essay on Criticism used in this paper is that of An Oxford Anthology of English Poetry, 2d ed., ed. Howard Foster Lowry and Willard Thorp (New York, 1956), pp. 413–422.

Parenthetical reference in the text is preferable to the piling up of many footnotes, and you had better use it when you make many references to one book. And in literary studies you may have other decisions to make. Assume you are writing on Nathaniel Hawthorne's tales. Unless you are writing a most minute study, you will hardly need page reference. You will use the names of the tales in your text, and the tales are not so long that the reader cannot find the passages you quote or discuss in any edition he happens to have. Or, if you were working with Twain's *Adventures of Huckleberry Finn*, might not reference by chapter be better than page reference? The chapter numbers will be the same in all editions. Type chapter numbers in roman numerals or in arabic numbers, whichever they are in the source; for roman numerals use lower case letters (Chapter xxvi). Whether or not you use parenthetical documentation in the final form of your paper, you will do well to use it in draft copies. One is far less likely to omit or confuse documentation if he includes it from the beginning.

Footnotes and Footnote Numbers

Often all the documentation cannot well be done within the text, and footnotes are necessary. Long parenthetical references may be awkward in the text, and several of them close together highly distracting for the reader. "Let the test be," *The MLA Style Sheet* says, "whether or not [the reference] interferes seriously with ease in reading." If it does, put it in a footnote. As things work out in practice, one is likely to make his page references to his major primary sources in parentheses within the text, and to use footnotes for his other sources.

Beginning source paper writers have a tendency to use more footnotes than are necessary in some places in their papers and to omit them when they are necessary in others. If, for instance, you use three short quotations from one source within a single paragraph of your text, one footnote (with its index number after the last quotation) will generally take care of all three—although one footnote will not document more than one paragraph. If your reader, with no great trouble can take your work back to your sources, your footnoting is adequate. But do remember that documentation indicates the relationship of all your work to your sources, and that it is just as necessary, therefore, to document a summary restatement of a passage as it is a quotation. The illustrative passages in the next two chapters will adequately represent the occasions for documentation. When you come to them, notice how the number of footnotes is held down.

Basic Conventions for Footnotes. The conventions for footnote references are designed to maintain consistency in documentation. As you check the examples below against your own footnotes, try to see the logic in the forms they use. The index at the back of this book will help you to check details.

In a footnote the author's first name appears first. (Remember that bibliographies, arranged in alphabetical order, put the author's last name first.) Items in a footnote are separated by commas, instead of periods, as in a bibliographical entry; and the publisher's name (when included) is separated from the city of publication by a colon. Volume numbers for books are in roman numerals, and pages in arabic numerals. The abbreviations p. and pp. are used for "page" and "pages," and vol. for "volume." If, however, both volume and page are cited in a footnote, both abbreviations are omitted: II, 207. The principle holds for all footnotes.

Footnotes are numbered with superior (raised) figures and the index numbers for them in the text are also superior figures — like this.[10] The index number in the text is placed *after* the quotation from the source, or the restatement or discussion of the source, so that the position of the number indicates where the dependence on a particular source ends in a given paragraph. In the source paper, footnotes are numbered consecutively through the paper. We are assuming the usual practice in which footnotes appear at the bottom of the page to which they refer, but they may appear grouped together at the end of the paper (see page 53).

Footnote References to Books

This section illustrates all the footnote forms for references to books that you are likely to need, and intends to make clear the logic of the practices illustrated. When you come to writing your paper, you should check your footnotes against the examples until you are confident about the forms. The index to this book will lead you to any detail you may be doubtful about. And the first item in the index is a list of abbreviations, including some that are not used in this book but that you may encounter in your sources.

First Reference When All Information Appears in the Footnote. The information required in a first footnote reference is the information necessary to identify the book, unless — as often — the writer's full name appears in the text. The information required is just that of the bibliography card, except that the footnote includes a page reference, and that the publisher's name may be omitted with ordinary, easy-to-identify books. You will remember that bibliographical information is taken from the title page and — often for the date of publication — the copyright page. In a footnote, the writer's name appears in normal order; the punctuation and abbreviations are best learned by paying attention to the examples. The following examples will give models for most books to which you will make footnote reference.

1. Form including publisher's name. The second edition of the *MLA Style Sheet* recommends the inclusion of the publisher's name in first footnote references. This example shows a book for which there is a sample bibliography card on page 8 so that you may compare bibliography and footnote form:

    [10]Louis C. Hunter, <u>Steamboats on the Western Rivers</u> (Cambridge, Mass.: Harvard University Press, 1949), pp. 287–288.

Your instructor may prefer that you always include the publisher's name. Certainly it should be included whenever, for any reason, a book is hard to find or identify. Here are first footnote references to a rare book,[1] a book for which the date is not ascertainable[2] (note the handling of two authors), and a paperback reprint of an often-reprinted book[3] (with the publisher's name for the series included for identification).

¹Washington Irving, A Book of the Hudson (New York: G. P. Putnam, 1849), p. 115.
²Algernon B. Gothland and Cecil K. Cockloft, Metrical Studies (Baltimore: Banal and Prim, n.d.), pp. 65–70.
³Nathaniel Hawthorne, The Scarlet Letter (The Library of Literature; Indianapolis: Bobbs–Merrill, 1963), p. 133.

2. Form without publisher's name. For most books used by undergraduates in course papers, the publisher's name is hardly necessary. As the *MLA Style Sheet* points out, scholars using easy-to-identify books commonly omit the publisher's name in first footnote references.

¹Alvin F. Harlow, Old Towpaths (New York, 1926), p. 364.

Most of the first footnote references in our textbook do omit the name of the publisher, since the books used are easy to identify. When the publisher's name is included, it is to identify an edition or reprint.

First Reference When Author's Full Name Appears in the Text. If the author's full name is used in the text, it is not used in the footnote (but the title appears in the footnote even if it has been used in the text).

¹Old Towpaths (New York, 1926), p. 364.

Footnote References After the First. For a second footnote reference to a book (or any number of subsequent footnote references) use the author's last name — or author's name and short title — and page number or numbers.

¹¹Hunter, p. 290. [or] ¹¹Hunter, Steamboats, p. 290.

The first form is usually entirely adequate. But if, for example, you were using two books by Louis C. Hunter, or one by him and one by John K. Hunter, you would need the second form. The second form is also to be used when the reference is a long way from the first reference to the book. If there are two authors, use both names: Gothland and Cockloft, p. 7.

Of the abbreviations for certain Latin words that used to be used in footnote references subsequent to the first to stand for titles, only one is surviving today: Ibid. It stands for *ibidem* ("in the same place"). It may be used immediately following a footnote that identifies the source in hand. But it must follow on the same page of the paper. It may be repeated on that same page as long as no other footnote reference to another source intervenes.

⁶George Rogers Taylor, The Transportation Revolution 1815–1860 (New York, 1951), pp. 141–142.
⁷Ibid., p. 155.
⁸Ibid.

But nothing much is gained thereby, and "Taylor, p. 155" is clearer. The only real advantage that Ibid. ever has is illustrated by footnote 8 above, where the reference is to the same book *and* the same page as the reference made by footnote 7. Notice that Ibid. is not underlined.

Footnote References to Translated and Edited Books. These forms, which are a little more complex, and which you will probably use infrequently, will need careful checking in your paper.

1. A translated work.

[7]Albert Camus, <u>Notebooks</u> <u>1939</u>-<u>1942</u>, trans. Philip Thedy (New York, 1963), p. 197.

2. A volume from a collected works with an editor.

[9]<u>The</u> <u>Works</u> <u>of</u> <u>Rufus</u> <u>Choate</u>, ed. S. G. Brown (Boston, 1862), I, 356.

The principle that when the writer's name is given in the text it need not be repeated in the footnote holds even here; if Choate were named in the text the footnote would be written thus: [9]*Works*, ed. S. G. Brown (Boston, 1862), I, 356. A reference subsequent to the first would be this: Choate, I, 360. Remember the principle that when both volume and page numbers appear, no abbreviations are used.

3. A single item reprinted in a collection or an anthology.

[5]Allan R. Bosworth, "The Golden Age of Pulps," reprinted in <u>Writer</u> <u>to</u> <u>Reader</u>, ed. Neal Frank Doubleday (Boston, 1966), p. 319.

In practice this example would probably begin with the title of the article, for it is likely that the author's name would appear in the text. A reference subsequent to the first would be this: Bosworth, p. 320.

4. An essay included in a work with many authors and, in this example, more than three editors.

[6]Dixon Wector, "Literary Culture on the Frontier," <u>Literary</u> <u>History</u> <u>of</u> <u>the</u> <u>United</u> <u>States</u>, ed. Robert E. Spiller et al. (New York, 1948), II, 653.

Again, the author's name would probably appear in the text, so that the footnote would begin with the title of the essay. A footnote reference subsequent to the first begins with the name of the author of the essay rather than with the editor's name: Wecter, p. 654.

5. Footnote reference to the comment of an editor. There is one further consideration about footnotes to edited books. If you were referring, for instance, to a passage from John Henry Newman's *The Idea of a University* that you found in *Victorian Prose,* edited by Frederick William Roe, and you had included in your text Newman's name—as you normally would—the footnote would take this form:

[9]<u>The</u> <u>Idea</u> <u>of</u> <u>a</u> <u>University</u>, reprinted in part in <u>Victorian</u> <u>Prose,</u> ed. Frederick William Roe (New York, 1947), p. 193.

But if you had used in your text a passage that the editor had written, say in his headnote to his selections from Newman's work, the footnote would take this form:

    10Frederick William Roe, ed., <u>Victorian</u> <u>Prose</u> (New York, 1947), p. 159.

This footnote makes clear that the reference is to editorial comment, not to the work of one of the writers included in the collection. If you had used Professor Roe's name in your text, the footnote would start *Victorian Prose*. A reference to Professor Roe's editorial comment subsequent to the first may be simply this: Roe, p. 169.

The "Quoted in . . ." Footnote. When you have used a passage quoted in one of your sources, you must always footnote to the book from which you yourself have quoted. Suppose in a paper about Mark Twain, you quote a passage from Captain Basil Hall's *Travels in North America* you have found quoted in Hunter's *Steamboats on the Western Rivers*. You would attribute the passage to Hall in your text, and your footnote would be one of these, depending upon whether the reference to Hunter's book was a first reference or any subsequent one:

    12Quoted in Louis C. Hunter, <u>Steamboats</u> <u>on</u> <u>the</u> <u>Western</u> <u>Rivers</u> (Cambridge, Mass., 1949), p. 254.
    12Quoted in Hunter, p. 254.

Footnote Preparation for Within-text References

If you are to use documentation by parentheses within the text, you must be especially careful to identify the source fully when it is first cited. When there are to be a good many references, that opening identification is usually done by a preparatory footnote at the first reference to the source. This footnote must make clear how subsequent references are to be handled. Two examples of such footnotes were shown in the section called "Documentation Within the Text" above, but the examples below show more typical situations.

In Chapter 2 there was a discussion on how to handle a passage from *Life on the Mississippi*, and the page references were made parenthetically in the text. Since Mark Twain's name as the author of *Life on the Mississippi* would certainly appear in the text, the first reference to the book and the preparation for subsequent within-text references would appear as this footnote:

    1<u>Life</u> <u>on</u> <u>the</u> <u>Mississippi</u> (New York, 1950), p. 45. All subsequent page references to this book will appear parenthetically in the text.

For parenthetical documentation, use a good edition of the work—one that you are reasonably sure that your readers can find.

If the example in Chapter 2 had been using the *Life on the Mississippi* volume from a set of Mark Twain's works, the footnote would have been a little more extensive:

¹<u>Life</u> <u>on</u> <u>the</u> <u>Mississippi</u>, p. 42, in <u>The</u> <u>Writings</u> <u>of</u> <u>Mark</u>
<u>Twain,</u> Hillcrest Edition, New York: Harper & Brothers, 1904–
1907. Subsequent page references to this book will appear
parenthetically in the text.

Footnote preparation for parenthetical reference to an edition of Twain's letters would be this:

⁴<u>Mark</u> <u>Twain's</u> <u>Letters</u>, ed. Albert Bigelow Paine (New York,
1917), I, 43–44. Twain's letters will hereafter be referred
to by the volume and page numbers of this edition.

The form of the parenthetical reference would be simply (I, 46) or (II, 74). The
principle that no abbreviations are used with volume and page numbers when
both appear holds good everywhere.

As we have seen, writers often use parenthetical documentation for primary
sources and footnotes for secondary sources. The practice is extensively illustrated in the sample source paper in the last chapter of this book.

Footnote References to Periodicals

Footnote reference to periodicals differs from footnote reference to books
only as the conditions of periodical publication make necessary. First references to all periodicals include their dates, and first references to quarterly
and monthly publications include their volume numbers.

First Footnote References to Articles in Quarterly and Monthly Periodicals.
Scholarly and professional journals are usually published quarterly; but the
form for reference to articles in them does not differ essentially from the form
for monthly publications. The second edition of the *MLA Style Sheet* uses
arabic numerals for all volume numbers of periodicals, even when the
periodicals use roman numerals. If you have questions about changing roman
numerals to arabic numerals, consult the entry for "roman numerals" in a
good desk dictionary. (Roman numerals have long been used in footnote
references to periodicals, and you will see them so used in your sources.)

1. First reference when all of the information appears in the note.
   ³G. Harrison Orions, "The Angel of Hadley in Fiction," <u>Amer-</u>
<u>ican</u> <u>Literature</u>, 4 (November 1932), 257–269.
   ⁴Walter Blair, "When Was <u>Huckleberry</u> <u>Finn</u> Written?" <u>Amer-</u>
<u>ican</u> <u>Literature</u>, 30 (March 1958), 23.
   ⁵J. Edwin Wood, "The Venous System," <u>Scientific</u> <u>American</u>,
218 (January 1968), 86–96.
   ⁶T. S. Matthews, "The Rite of Summer," <u>American</u> <u>Scholar</u>, 39
(Summer 1970), 463–467.

Notice that when a title ends with a question mark or an exclamation point
no comma follows.

2. When the author's name appears in the text.

1"The Angel of Hadley in Fiction," American Literature, 4 (November 1932), 257–269.

3. Monthly magazines of recent date (within the last year or so), for which volume number may be omitted.

6Dan Wakefield, "Novel Bites Man," Atlantic Monthly, August 1970, pp. 72–78.

Footnote References Subsequent to the First for Articles in Periodicals. Subsequent reference is handled just as for books.

6Orions, p. 268.
7Wakefield, pp. 77–78.

Footnote References to Articles in Periodicals Appearing Oftener than Once a Month. For such periodicals a volume number is usually not given, but the day of publication is given.

15Robert Shaplen, "Letter from South Vietnam," The New Yorker, June 4, 1966, p. 142.
16"Trade: Dangerous Drift for the U.S.," Time, December 13, 1968, p. 89.
17Time, December 13, 1968, p. 89.

In news magazines there may be no author given; then, if the text has made clear the subject matter of the article, its title can usually be dispensed with, and the footnote may start with the name of the periodical.

Footnote References to Material in Newspapers. There is usually no author's name involved. If an article has an author and title (as distinct from headline) they will be handled just as for other periodicals. If the newspaper has separately paged sections, as frequently in Sunday editions, the form is this:

22New York Times, September 4, 1966, Sec. 1, p. 2.

Notice that the place name is not underlined. In newspapers in which the pages are numbered consecutively throughout, the form is this:

8Boston Globe, March 1, 1969, p. 1.
9Decatur [Illinois] Daily Review, June 18, 1966, p. 4.

A column number may be added, e.g., col. 3. The name of the state is added in brackets only when the reader may not recognize the name of the city, or when he may confuse it with another city of the same name in another state. When the name of the newspaper does not include a place name, it may be added in parentheses, e.g., *Christian Science Monitor* (Boston).

Supporting Footnotes

Scholars and research writers often use footnotes for purposes beyond documentation — to extend their texts in various ways. You had better not do much of that; you should generally assume that what cannot be worked into your text is better omitted. But there is one sort of note written to support an assertion in the text that you may occasionally find convenient. Here is a passage from page 275 of Hunter's *Steamboats on the Western Rivers* and its accompanying footnote:

> The "other obstructions" frequently classed with snags as causes of accidents — rocks, sunken boats, and the like — led to the sinking of many steamboats and caused large aggregate damage but little loss of life.[9] Snags presented a different and more difficult problem because of their greater number, . . .

> [9]For example, in 1855 seventy-six steamboats were listed as sunk from various causes other than explosion, fire, or collision, with a total loss of five lives. By contrast, sixty-five were lost in the five explosions occurring in the year (Cincinnati *Gazette,* January 10, 1856).

Now of course the assertion made in the text could have been supported in the text, but that would have slowed up the discussion a little. The footnote supports the assertion and helps to move the discussion along. Notice how the parenthetical documentation is handled within the footnote. You will find comparable footnotes in the sample paper in the last chapter of this book.

Text and Documentation on the Page

On page 54 there is a sample source paper page with footnotes. And the sample source paper beginning on page 104 illustrates matters of form. The usual practices for placement and general form are these: (a) On an 8½ × 11 page there should be generous margins — 1½ inches top and left, and one inch bottom and right. Of course the bottom margin may turn out to be a little more than an inch. And for the first page of the paper, the distance between top and title should be about 2 inches (with no page number). Triple space is used between title and text. (b) The page number appears at the upper right, an arabic number, *not* followed by a period. (c) Footnotes are separated from the text by an extra line of space. It is sometimes recommended that footnote be separated from the text by a line. It is here urged that no line be used ordinarily, and that a typed line one space below the text be used *only* to separate text and a footnote that has been continued to a second page (the occasion for such a continued footnote will be rare).

A little planning saves trouble in typing. Footnotes in your papers will probably not average as many as four a page, but it will save time if you can foresee the pages on which footnotes concentrate, and watch the space. Then, too, you will want to avoid breaking quoted matter awkwardly at the end of a page. Do not end a page with the title of a poem, or with only a line or two of a stanza or verse or of a passage in blank verse. And do not carry over to the following page a single line of a single-spaced quotation. Prefer leaving pages short.

Form for Manuscript Prepared as if Intended for Publication. There is
another form you may use if your instructor approves. In this form the manuscript is prepared just as manuscripts submitted for publication are prepared
for the printer. Such a manuscript differs from the examples in this textbook
only in two ways.

In the first place, prose quotations of less than 100 words are run into
the text, in quotation marks, of course. Prose quotations of a 100 words
or more are separated from the text by two extra lines of space and double-
spaced. They are typed full width or indented slightly (say three spaces)
from the left margin. If typed full width, they may be marked off by a neat
vertical line drawn beside them along the left margin. Verse quotations are
handled as you have been directed, except that they are double-spaced.

In the second place, footnotes in such a manuscript come at the end of
the paper and are double-spaced. They begin on a new page. Here, as examples, are some selected footnotes from the sample paper that begins on
page 104, set up as they would be in a manuscript intended for publication.

3
Ronald E. Shaw, Erie Water West (Lexington, Ky., 1966),

p. 214.

4
A Boy's Town (New York, 1890), pp. 238–241.

7
Quoted in Shaw, p. 209.

9
Mosses from an Old Manse, p. 485, in Works, Riverside Edi-

tion, Boston: Houghton, Mifflin and Company, 1883. Subsequent

page references to "The Canal Boat" will appear parenthet-

ically in the text.

11
Along the Erie every farmer whose land was divided by the

canal had a bridge built for him by the State of New York. See

Adams, pp. 71–72.

A Page with Footnote Documentation

"'Let the storm increase,' said Rugg, with a fearful oath,
'I will see home to-night, in spite of the last tempest, or may
I never see home!'"6 This near repetition of the wish of the
skipper of the Flying Dutchman was quite as disastrous as the
skipper's wish, and Peter Rugg wanders yet in the American imagination.

Indeed, later writers have used the tale much as they might
have used a folk tradition, and made it their own much as Austin made the Flying Dutchman legend his own. There is a treatment of it in verse by Amy Lowell (who says she knew an oral
version long before she ever heard of Austin).7 And we learn
in Frank Luther Mott's 1950 Saturday Evening Post story "Phan-
tom Flivver" that Peter Rugg has traveled in a Model T Ford on
Kansas roads.8 But long before the Model T, the Flying Dutchman
legend had a Mississippi river version: Mark Twain tells of
two pilots, lost in a bend of the river generally unused since
a new cut-off had formed, who "fell to swearing and finally uttered the entirely unnecessary wish that they might never get
out of that place," and whose boat was in Twain's river days
still seen wandering on dismal nights in that forgotten elbow
of the river.9 We do not know the name of either pilot; perhaps
one of them was called Rugg.

6"Peter Rugg, the Missing Man," p. 217.
7Legends (Boston, 1921), pp. 238–252. See "Preface," p. xiii.
8Saturday Evening Post Stories 1950 (New York, 1950), pp.
155–165.
9Life on the Mississippi (New York, 1950), p. 158.

6 problems in the use of sources

This chapter will illustrate five patterns in the use of sources, each for a defined purpose. The problems that emerge—so far as they are problems of approach and method—are in no way special. A student will encounter them, or some of them, in his first source paper.

The Economical Use of a Secondary Source

Classroom experience shows that secondary sources present more difficulties for students than do primary sources. Suppose, for example, that the student who worked on an Adams-Jefferson paper in Chapter 2 is now expanding that paper into an extended discussion of the political and social thought of the two men. In the first part of his paper he is, quite rightly, concerned with some initial generalization about the development of Adams' political thought. Reading some secondary works, he finds the following passage useful.

From Vernon Louis Parrington, *The Colonial Mind 1620–1800*. New York: Harcourt, Brace and Company, 1927.

308   During the revolutionary struggle he had been a member of the left wing; during the early struggles under the Constitution he was a member of the right wing. The young man had been a stalwart defender of human rights, the old man was a stalwart defender of property rights; and this shift of position was fatal to his reputation with the rising democratic party. The French Revolution marked the critical turning point in his intellectual development. As a politician he was well-nigh ruined by it; but as a political thinker he owed it much. Before that vast upheaval came to challenge his somewhat conventional mind, he was a hard-working lawyer-politician, with a liking for legalistic constitutional theory; but as the Revolution went forward, he was forced into uncompromising reaction.

The student at work here understands that direct quotation will ordinarily be limited to passages from his primary sources; he intends to use this passage, therefore, only in summary restatement. He remembers and puts into practice a principle of summary: Make your own statement; do not patch together phrases from the original. He writes:

> V. L. Parrington believes that the French Revolution was the turning point in the development of Adams' political views. He says that, although Adams had been considered a member of the left wing in his advocacy of the American Revolution, the French Revolution forced him to consider his political principles anew, and that he reached a position of "uncompromising reaction."[2]

> [2]The Colonial Mind 1620–1800 (New York, 1927), p. 308.

The student has rightly included Parrington's name in his restatement, for the passage makes a judgment (if the passage were merely recording undisputed fact, that would be unnecessary). Possibly, however, he used more space than he could afford. He might reduce the passage this way:

> V. L. Parrington believes that the French Revolution forced Adams to reconsider his liberal political principles, and that he reached a position of "uncompromising reaction."[2]

The purpose of this student's paper justifies a use of his secondary source; there are even rare occasions when direct quotation from a secondary source is justified. But students must beware: too much use of secondary material will make a paper seem to be written around instead of on a topic. At worst, a paper may become a rehash of almost plagiarized material.

Careful consideration must therefore be given both to economy and to ethics in restatement. Now the sample restatement above may seem simple enough, but its formulation requires skills that are often not easy to learn. Reducing source materials properly is such an important matter that perhaps this time an illustration is needed of what should *not* be done. Assume that another student is working on the same Parrington passage and produces the following paragraph, which purports to be a restatement of it.

> During the revolution Adams had been a member of the left wing, but in the early struggles under the constitution he was a member of the right wing. The young man had been a stalwart defender of human rights; the old man was a stalwart defender of property rights. The French Revolution marked a turning point in his intellectual development, for although as a politician he was nearly ruined by it, he owed it much as a political thinker. Earlier he was a hard-working lawyer and politician who liked constitutional theory, but as the Revolution went forward, he was forced into uncompromising reaction.

What has this unfortunate fellow done? He has made an entirely improper use of his source, he has produced a queer hybrid sort of passage—neither quotation nor restatement, but a patchwork of both—and he has failed to attain any considerable reduction. When he came to his paper, he forgot everything he had learned about summary. Had he used quotation marks around the parts of sentences lifted bodily from Parrington's text, he would have avoided the semi-plagiarism with which he is chargeable; his passage would have been honest, if ineffectual.

This student's trouble has its inception during his notetaking. Obviously he half copied the Parrington passage without thinking what he was doing, and of course he is unable to tell, when he comes to use the note, what is quoted and what is not.

A Secondary Source Used for Background

Suppose that a student is writing a paper on the problem of air pollution in his own medium-sized Middle Western city. There has been new state legislation that has forced local industries to install equipment to reduce the amount of pollutants they throw into the atmosphere. A report of a local commission to study air pollution has recently been released, and there has been much newspaper discussion. The student, therefore, has a good deal of local material. But in the first part of his paper he needs to discuss the problem in general, to see how far the local problem is like the national one (see the discussion of the analysis of problems in Chapter 4). The student finds the following paragraphs useful to his purpose.

From Walsh McDermott, "Air Pollution and Public Health," *Scientific American*, 205 (October 1961), 49–57.

51   In metropolitan regions all over the country municipal installations, households, industrial plants and automobiles (to list them in ascending order of rank as sources of pollution) give off approximately the same combination and relative volume of chemicals to the air. Whether the contamination becomes a community problem at any one time depends on population density and the weather. The strong breezes that attend the movement of great air masses over the continent regularly bring fresh air into most U.S. cities, and in the absence of breezes the air may be cleaned by updrafts that dilute and carry away both the smoke and the vaporized chemicals. Not infrequently these natural ventilation processes fail, and there may be no movement of air over a particular area for a matter of hours and sometimes days. One mechanism that stops air movement is the "thermal inversion." Ordinarily the air is warmer at the ground and colder above; indeed, the updrafts so
52 essential for air cleansing arise from this temperature gradient. In / a thermal inversion a layer of warm air forms at higher altitude and traps a layer of cold air at the ground. When an inversion roofs over the atmosphere of a heavily populated region, the same air must accumulate a much higher concentration of pollutants. This can happen in almost any season of the year to most of the cities in this country; it is the chronic situation in Los Angeles.

Los Angeles suffers from its smogs not because its natives are unusually careless but because there are so many of them in a place where the cleansing of the air is so frequently interrupted. There six million people with three million cars burn 5.5 million gallons of gasoline each day on a narrow strip of sunny seacoast backed up by mountains. Thermal inversions occur about 100 days each year. The Los Angeles case may seem extreme, and it is the extreme at this moment. But two of the three factors that prevail there—rapid population growth and heavy hydrocarbon emission—are not peculiar to Los Angeles. The third factor—thermal inversion—can come into play elsewhere as well. What has happened to Los Angeles, therefore, is already happening to certain other urban regions and may have considerable future significance for the nation as a whole. . . .

54   The aggravation of chronic bronchitis-emphysema by air pollution has been most drastically demonstrated in the few epidemics of acute illness attributed to air pollution. In the cases of the Donora "disaster" and the London episode of 1952 the evidence is decisive. The air at Donora, on a bend of the Monongahela River with high hills on all sides, must take up the smoke and fume of blast furnaces, steel mills, sulfuric acid mills and slag-processing plants. In October, 1948, a thermal inversion occurred over most of the U.S., including the Donora basin. There the usual smog, instead of lifting each day at noon as was its custom, remained unabated. By the third day of constant smog, 5,910 persons were reported ill. More than 60 per cent of the inhabitants 65 and older were affected, and almost half of these were seriously ill. In all, 20 persons died, 17 of the deaths occurring on the third day of unremitting smog. Then a heavy rain fell, the smog disappeared and the epidemic stopped immediately. In London in 1952 there was an "excess" mortality of 4,000 to 5,000 persons during one week. The deaths in both London and Donora occurred almost exclusively among those with previous bronchopulmonary disease. Indeed, the veteran bronchitis patients in the London clinics served almost as the canaries that miners once carried to detect noxious gases: they noted discomfort six to 12 hours before it was evident to others that an episode of smog was at hand.

For the purposes of his paper, the student might draw from the passage a paragraph like this:

In this country the classic examples of air pollution are the Donora disaster and the continual difficulty with smog in Los Angeles. Donora is on the Monongahela River in Pennsylvania, and is surrounded by hills. In October of 1948, as a result of a thermal inversion which held down the pollutants usually carried away by up-draft, twenty persons died there and 5,910 were reported as ill.[3] The smog in Los Angeles, about which everyone has heard, is a particularly serious problem because of the great number of automobiles operating on a narrow strip of land between the mountains and the sea in a region where thermal inversions are frequent, occurring about 100 days in each year.[4]

Thermal inversions are relatively infrequent over our city, and we have no hills or mountains to hold pollutants as in a cup. But we . . .

[3]Walsh McDermott, "Air Pollution and Public Health," Scientific American, 205 (October 1961), 54.
    [4]McDermott, p. 52.

Although the student has of course footnoted his paragraph, he has not named the writer of his source in his text. In this instance his practice is proper, for what Professor McDermott has said about Donora and Los Angeles is what one might find in several places; the parts of the source passage used do not include interpretation or conclusion in any way particularly his. Had the student used Professor McDermott's definition of "thermal inversion," or any of his interpretations or conclusions, his name ought to have appeared in the text of the paper. However, if you are at any time in real doubt about including the name of the writer of a source in your text, include it — it will do no harm.

A Source with a Difficult Style

When you are handling a source with a special or mannered style, you need to take care that your own style is not colored by it. Except when you are quoting, the style in your paper should be your style. The more mannered the style of a source is, the more likely a student using it is to pick up some of its characteristics. To illustrate the problem, consider a paragraph from Thorstein Veblen's *The Theory of the Leisure Class* (1899). It is a classic, but Veblen writes in his kind of jargon and in persistent abstraction, and he has a habit of giving a new and special sense to familiar words.

Chapter 4 considered the planning of a paper concerned with the appeals made to housewives by both the articles and advertisements in household magazines. Now assume that a student in his reading for that paper has come to realize that much that has been written recently about status and status symbols had been said by Veblen, but in his terms, about seventy years ago.

From Thorstein Veblen, *The Theory of the Leisure Class,* reprinted in *The Portable Veblen,* ed. Max Lerner. New York: The Viking Press, 1948.

125   The basis on which good repute in any highly organized industrial community ultimately rests is pecuniary strength; and the means of showing pecuniary strength, and so of gaining or retaining a good name, are leisure and a conspicuous consumption of goods. Accordingly, both of these methods are in vogue as far down 126 the scale as it remains possible; and in the lower strata in / which the two methods are employed, both offices are in great part delegated to the wife and children of the household. Lower still, where any degree of leisure, even ostensible, has become impracticable for the wife, the conspicuous consumption of goods remains and is carried on by the wife and children. The man of the household also can do something in this direction, and, indeed, he commonly does; but with a still lower descent into the levels of indigence — along the margin of the slums — the man, and presently also the children, virtually cease to consume valuable goods for appearances, and the woman remains virtually the sole exponent of the household's pecuniary decency. No class of society, not even the most abjectly poor, forgoes all customary conspicuous consumption. The last items of this category of consumption are not given up except under the stress of the direst necessity. Very much of squalor and discomfort will be endured before the last trinket or the last pretence of pecuniary decency is put away. There is no class and no coun-

try that has yielded so abjectly before the pressure of physical want as to deny themselves all gratification of this higher or spiritual need.

This student is using Veblen's book in the library, and in writing the paper he will be depending upon his note cards. He must be sure that his notes are clear to himself, and that they do not betray him into a poor parody of Veblen's style. And with Veblen he has another problem. Although the one paragraph is all he plans to use, of course it must be understood in context. He has read enough of *The Theory of the Leisure Class* to understand what "leisure" and "conspicuous consumption" (key terms in the book) mean; he sees that his first note should establish them. (Since he is taking only these notes on Veblen's book, he will not need a subject heading.)

Veblen, p. 125

"The basis on which good repute in any highly organized industrial community ultimately rests is pecuniary strength; and the means of showing pecuniary strength, and so of gaining or retaining a good name, are leisure and a conspicuous consumption of goods."

"leisure" (elsewhere "conspicuous leisure") = activity of any obvious sort that does not bring a money return.

"conspicuous consumption"—the possession and use of goods at least partly for the impression they make on others.

The next card follows the development of the paragraph in part, but the student does not need to make a complete précis.

Veblen, p. 126
continued

(a) A man does what he can to display his wealth, but he is usually busy making the money, and most display must be done by the wife.

(b) If a family has so little money that the wife can't display "leisure," she (and the children) yet can do something about "conspicuous consumption."

(c) The less money the family has, the more the duty of maintaining family status ("pecuniary decency") falls upon the wife alone.

The student has taken notes for his purpose, and notes that he can trust. They put in capsule form the definitions of crucial terms without relying on the peculiar vocabulary of the author. And they summarize the main points of the paragraph. Because the student has freed himself from Veblen's jargon at this point, his notes go rather easily into his paper.

The reason that so much promotion and advertising direct their appeals to women was made clear long ago in Thorstein Veblen's The Theory of the Leisure Class (1899). Veblen points out that in an industrialized society status depends upon what he calls "conspicuous consumption"–the possession and use of goods that give an impression of wealth; and upon "conspicuous leisure"–activity of any obvious sort that yields no money reward. According to Veblen, this display of wealth (except among the very rich) is largely, and in some families almost entirely, the duty of the wife. If she cannot do very much about a display of conspicuous leisure, she will yet manage the conspicuous consumption on which the family status depends.[7]

However much things have changed in seventy years, Veblen's principle is still recognized in the articles and the advertisements in the magazines we are considering. An analysis of . . .

[7]The Portable Veblen, ed. Max Lerner (New York: The Viking Press, 1948), pp. 125–126.

Notice how the student keeps it clear that the whole of his first paragraph depends on Veblen. In the second paragraph, his use of "we" is proper, since the pronoun does include both writer and readers. But avoid the editorial "we" in a source paper, or the use of "we" as a pretentious substitute for "I." The student has done well to include the date of the first publication of *The Theory of the Leisure Class;* most students need to be reminded to be clear about dates and periods.

The Economical Use of a Substantial Passage

The following source passage will be the basis of examples to show flexible and economical adaptation of a source to the purpose of a writer. This passage has a rather loose organization, one that might offer a source paper writer some difficulty. It will be used, moreover, in brief treatments and for specific purposes. It is the third letter from St. John de Crèvecoeur's *Letters from an American Farmer* (1782).[1]

[1]Crèvecoeur (1735–1813) was born in France and emigrated first to Canada and then to New York. The *Letters*, written for European readers, were based on Crèvecoeur's experience in Orange County in colonial New York during the decade before the Revolution. When the Revolution came, Crèvecoeur was a loyalist, perhaps because he could not see that Americans had any real reason for revolt. The *Letters* are a valuable record and might be part of the reading in college courses in literature or history.

From J. Hector St. John de Crevecoeur, "What is an American?" *Letters from an American Farmer*. New York: Fox, Duffield & Company, 1904.

49   We are a people of cultivators, scattered over an immense territory, communicating with each other by means of good roads and navigable rivers, united by the silken bands of mild government, all respecting the laws, without dreading their power, because they are equitable. We are all animated with the spirit of
50   an industry which is / unfettered and unrestrained, because each person works for himself. If he travels through our rural districts he views not the hostile castle, and the haughty mansion, contrasted with the clay-built hut and miserable cabin, where cattle and men help to keep each other warm, and dwell in meanness, smoke and indigence. A pleasing uniformity of decent competence appears throughout our habitations. The meanest of our log-houses is a dry and comfortable habitation. Lawyer or merchant are the fairest titles our towns afford; that of a farmer is the only appellation of the rural inhabitants of our country. It must take some time ere he can reconcile himself to our dictionary, which is but short in words of dignity, and names of honour. There, on a Sunday, he sees a congregation of respectable farmers and their wives, all clad in neat homespun, well mounted, or riding in their own humble waggons. There is not among them an esquire, saving the unlettered magistrate. There he sees a parson as simple as his flock, a farmer who does not riot on the labour of others. We have no princes, for whom we toil, starve, and bleed: we are the most perfect society now existing in the world. Here man is free as he ought to be; nor is this pleasing equality so transitory as
51   many others are. Many ages / will not see the shores of our great lakes replenished with inland nations, nor the unknown bounds of North America entirely peopled. Who can tell how far it extends? Who can tell the millions of men whom it will feed and contain? for no European foot has as yet travelled half the extent of this mighty continent!
     The next wish of this traveller will be to know whence came all these people? they are a mixture of English, Scotch, Irish, French, Dutch, Germans, and Swedes. From this promiscuous breed, that race now called Americans have arisen. The eastern provinces must indeed be excepted, as being the unmixed descendants of Englishmen. I have heard many wish that they had been more intermixed also: for my part, I am no wisher, and think it much better as it has happened. They exhibit a most conspicuous figure in this great and variegated picture; they too enter for a great share in the pleasing perspective displayed in these thirteen provinces. I know it is fashionable to reflect on them, but I respect them for what they have done; for the accuracy and wisdom with which they have settled their territory; for the decency of their manners; for their early love of letters; their ancient
52   college, the first in this hemisphere; for their industry; / which to me who am but a farmer, is the criterion of everything. There never was a people, situated as they are, who with so ungrateful a soil have done more in so short a time. Do you think that the monarchical ingredients which are more prevalent in other governments, have purged them from all foul stains? Their histories assert the contrary.
     In this great American asylum, the poor of Europe have by some means met together, and in consequence of various causes; to what purpose should they ask one another what countrymen they are? Alas, two thirds of them had no country. Can a wretch who wanders about, who works and starves, whose life is a continual

scene of sore affliction or pinching penury; can that man call England or any other kingdom his country? A country that had no bread for him, whose fields procured him no harvest, who met with nothing but the frowns of the rich, the severity of the laws, with jails and punishments; who owned not a single foot of the extensive surface of this planet? No! urged by a variety of motives, here they came. Every thing has tended to regenerate them; new laws, a new mode of living, a new social system; here they are become men: in Europe they were as so many useless plants, wanting vegetative mould, and / refreshing showers; they withered, and were mowed down by want, hunger, and war; but now by the power of transplantation, like all other plants they have taken root and flourished! Formerly they were not numbered in any civil lists of their country, except in those of the poor; here they rank as citizens. By what invisible power has this surprising metamorphosis been performed? By that of the laws and that of their industry. The laws, the indulgent laws, protect them as they arrive, stamping on them the symbol of adoption; they receive ample rewards for their labours; these accumulated rewards procure them lands; those lands confer on them the title of freemen, and to that title every benefit is affixed which men can possibly require. This is the great operation daily performed by our laws. From whence proceed these laws? From our government. Whence the government? It is derived from the original genius and strong desire of the people ratified and confirmed by the crown. This is the great chain which links us all, this is the picture which every province exhibits, Nova Scotia excepted. There the crown has done all; either there were no people who had genius, or it was not much attended to: the consequence is, that the province is very thinly inhabited indeed; the power of the crown / in conjunction with the musketos has prevented men from settling there. Yet some parts of it flourished once, and it contained a mild harmless set of people. But for the fault of a few leaders, the whole were banished. The greatest political error the crown ever committed in America, was to cut off men from a country which wanted nothing but men!

What attachment can a poor European emigrant have for a country where he had nothing? The knowledge of the language, the love of a few kindred as poor as himself, were the only cords that tied him: his country is now that which gives him land, bread, protection, and consequence. *Ubi panis ibi patria,* is the motto of all emigrants. What then is the American, this new man? He is either an European, or the descendant of an European, hence that strange mixture of blood, which you will find in no other country. I could point out to you a family whose grandfather was an Englishman, whose wife was Dutch, whose son married a French woman, and whose present four sons have now four wives of different nations. *He* is an American, who, leaving behind him all his ancient prejudices and manners, receives new ones from the new mode of life he has embraced, the new government he obeys, and the new rank he holds. / He becomes an American by being received in the broad lap of our great *Alma Mater.* Here individuals of all nations are melted into a new race of men, whose labours and posterity will one day cause great changes in the world. Americans are the western pilgrims, who are carrying along with them that great mass of arts, sciences, vigour, and industry which began long since in the east; they will finish the great circle. The Americans were once scattered all over Europe; here they are incorporated into one of the finest systems of population which has ever appeared, and which will hereafter become distinct by the power of the different climates they inhabit. The American ought therefore to love this country much better than that wherein either

The marginal line numbers 53, 54, 55 appear beside the corresponding lines.

he or his forefathers were born. Here the rewards of his industry follow with equal steps the progress of his labour; his labour is founded on the basis of nature, *self-interest;* can it want a stronger allurement? Wives and children, who before in vain demanded of him a morsel of bread, now, fat and frolicsome, gladly help their father to clear those fields whence exuberant crops are to arise to feed and to clothe them all; without any part being claimed, either by a despotic prince, a 56 rich abbot, or a mighty lord. Here religion demands but little of him; / a small voluntary salary to the minister, and gratitude to God; can he refuse these? The American is a new man, who acts upon new principles; he must therefore entertain new ideas, and form new opinions. From involuntary idleness, servile dependence, penury, and useless labour, he has passed to toils of a very different nature, rewarded by ample subsistence. — This is an American. . . .

   Men are like plants; the goodness and flavour of the fruit proceeds from the peculiar soil and exposition in which they grow. We are nothing but what we derive from the air we breathe, the climate we inhabit, the government we obey, the system of religion we profess, and the nature of our employment.

Assume that this piece of source material is to be used in a paper on the national origin of the population of the American colonies in the years before the Revolution. The paper might be written for a course in American history. For such a paper Crèvecoeur, a first-hand observer, would be an important source. But the writer is not dealing with New York alone, and he has much material; he must use this source economically and compactly. He might write the paragraph below. Think of its first sentence as transition from a foregoing treatment of the population of the New England colonies.

Although the New England colonies remained English in temper and to a considerable extent in population, New York had a mixture of nationalities. About that mixture we have interesting testimony in "What is an American?"—one of the Letters from an American Farmer by St. John de Crevecoeur, himself a resident of Orange County, New York, in the decade before the Revolution. Crèvecoeur saw a new nationality developing in New York. When he answers his own question, "What then is the American, this new man?" he says: "He is either an European, or the descendant of an European, hence that strange mixture of blood, which you will find in no other country. I could point out to you a family whose grandfather was an Englishman, whose wife was Dutch, whose son married a French woman, and whose present four sons have now four wives of different nations." These different nations were evidently all nations of northern Europe. Crèvecoeur lists the "English, Scotch, Irish, French, Dutch, Germans, and Swedes" as the nationalities that were all "melted into a new race of men," retaining nothing of their "ancient prejudices and manners," and, indeed, almost no attachment of any kind to their European inheritance.[11]

   [11]Letters from an American Farmer (New York, 1904), pp. 49–56.

Perhaps this paragraph will illustrate these two things: selection from the source for the purpose of the paper (but all of these examples ought to illustrate that), and the way in which one may move about in source material. Students too often may be controlled not only by the phrasing but by the structure of their sources. Notice how the writer of the paragraph above, although his dependence is primarily upon the latter part of the source passage, moves back in it at his will.

The source is carefully established at the beginning of the paragraph. When the name of the source is used in the text, as it ought to be with a primary source, make sure you name the source before you begin drawing upon it. Ordinarily in the first reference to a primary source, one includes the date of its first publication. What is more important for the purpose of this paper is an indication of the time of Crèvecoeur's observations — considerably earlier than the publication of his book.

In this regard there is a caution to be made: students sometimes may be misled into thinking of a publication date as the time of writing, and may even write "written in" some particular year when all they know is a publication date, which may be a good deal later. This is an easily avoidable error, once one is aware of the possible difference in date.

In the example above, it was necessary only to select the material pertinent to the paper's purpose and to give it a little context. Now assume an ambitious paper to be called "Theories of the American Character: a Comparative Study." It would consider James Fenimore Cooper's *Notions of the Americans* (1828), George Santayana's *Character and Opinion in the United States* (1920), D. W. Brogan's *America in the Modern World* (1960), and other works of comparable intention, but it would almost inevitably consider "What is an American?" first. That consideration should be a selected account of the passage, designed to make Crèvecoeur's thought clear. Now Crèvecoeur is a diffuse writer, and his rhetoric is elaborate. If one tried to handle this passage by the ordinary methods of summary, he would write far too much — and space would be a problem in this paper. The handling of "What is an American?" will have to be an account, not so much of Crevecoeur's text, as of his thinking; and it will require, first of all, careful reading.

See if you think the following account of the passage from "What is an American?" would serve its purpose in the paper we are assuming.

Although St. John de Crèvecoeur wrote his "What is an American?" one of the Letters from an American Farmer, in the decade before the Revolution, he describes in it the development of a distinct American character. He finds his emerging type of American in Orange County in colonial New York. This American is in no way a development of the European tradition, and perhaps he could not be found in New England. He is a farmer; he comes from northern Europe, or his immediate forebears did. He may have had parents of different nationalities; he is likely to be married to a woman of different national origin from his own. This mixture of nationalities, and the influence of an environment in which the citizens have both an economic and cultural equality, make the American, Crèvecoeur

insists, "a new man": "He is an American, who, leaving behind him
all his ancient prejudices and manners, receives new ones from the
new mode of life he has embraced, the new government he obeys, and
the new rank he holds."[1]

Crèvecoeur's central contention, indeed, is that the American
is a man made new by a new environment. The European who has become
an American "by the power of transplantation" retains, so far as
his character is concerned, nothing of the European tradition, nor
cares to; his inheritance hardly matters. "What attachment,"
Crèvecoeur asks, "can a poor European emigrant have for a country
where he had nothing?" The basis of the American's loyalty is self-
interest—a quite sufficient basis, Crèvecoeur thinks. And the
new man takes his nature from his place: "Men are like plants; the
goodness and flavour of the fruit proceeds from the peculiar soil
and exposition in which they grow."[2] Crèvecoeur's American, this
new man, is a new Adam, for whom the world itself is new.

[1]*Letters from an American Farmer* (New York, 1904), pp.
49–56.
[2]Ibid.

You will have noticed that the example, except for its first clause, is written
in the present tense throughout. If Crèvecoeur had been writing in the present
tense of particular persons in his time, then the example would have been
written in the past tense, of course. But since his American is a generalized
type, and since what Crèvecoeur says of him is Crevecoeur's doctrine, the
present tense is convenient and proper enough. You will not be able to estimate
how adequate this example passage is unless you take it back to Crèvecoeur's
text. For instance, is there a basis in that text for what is said in the example
passage of the cultural equality of Americans? Are the quotations well chosen?

Two footnotes are used, since a footnote to the second paragraph alone
would not clearly indicate the dependence of the first. The index number for
footnote 2 is placed as it is because the last sentence is not drawn from Crevecoeur, and is the comment of the writer of the example passage. Footnote 2
illustrates the convenience of "Ibid." in this somewhat unusual footnoting.

Use of a Literary Source

In using a literary source, a writer must be particularly careful to make his
point clear to readers who may not have read the source. This passage from
Henry David Thoreau's essay "Walking" (1862) would have its most obvious
source paper use in a discussion of the Westward movement, and for that it
will be considered here. It is reproduced below with considerable excision,
excision that concentrates it on the Westward theme. It is perhaps easier to
handle as presented here than it would be in its full form, for in the excision
some of the work that would ordinarily be done by the writer of the source
paper is done for him.

From Henry David Thoreau, "Walking," as reprinted in *Writer to Reader,* ed. Neal Frank Doubleday. Boston: D. C. Heath and Company, 1966.

38   When I go out of the house for a walk, uncertain as yet whither I will bend my steps, and submit myself to my instinct to decide for me, I find, strange and whimsical as it may seem, that I finally and inevitably settle southwest, toward some particular wood or meadow or deserted pasture or hill in that direction. My needle is slow to settle,—varies a few degrees, and does not always point due southwest, it is true, and it has good authority for this variation, but it always settles between west and south-southwest. The future lies that way to me, and the earth seems more unexhausted and richer on that side. . . . I turn round and round irresolute sometimes for a quarter of an hour, until I decide, for the thousandth time; that I will walk into the southwest or west. Eastward I go only by force; but westward I go free. Thither no business leads me. It is hard for me to believe that I shall find fair landscapes or sufficient wildness and freedom behind the eastern horizon. [8]I am not excited by the prospect of a walk thither; but I believe that the forest which I see in the western horizon stretches uninterruptedly toward the setting sun, and there are no towns nor cities in it of enough consequence to disturb me. [9]Let me live where I will, on this side is the city, on that the wilderness, and ever I am leaving the city more and more, and withdrawing into the wilderness. [10]I should not lay so much stress on this fact, if I did not believe that something like this is the prevailing tendency of my countrymen. [11]I must walk toward Oregon, and not toward Europe. And that way the nation is moving, and I may say that mankind progress from east to west. . . .

We go eastward to realise history and study the works of art and literature, retracing the steps of the race; we go westward as into the future, with a spirit of enterprise and adventure. [2]The Atlantic is a Lethean stream, in our passage over which we have had an opportunity to forget the Old World and its institutions. [3]If we do not succeed this time, there is perhaps one more chance for the race left before it arrives on the banks of the Styx; and that is in the Lethe of the Pacific, which is three times as wide.

I know not how significant it is, or how far it is an evidence of singularity, that an individual should thus consent in his pettiest walk with the general movement of the race; but I know that something akin to the migratory instinct in birds and quadrupeds . . . affects both nations and individuals, either perennially or from time to time. . . .

Every sunset which I witness inspires me with the desire to go to a West as distant and as fair as that into which the sun goes down. He appears to migrate westward daily, and tempts us to follow him. He is the Great Western Pioneer /
39 whom the nations follow. We dream all night of those mountain-ridges in the horizon, though they may be of vapor only, which were last gilded by his rays. The island of Atlantis, and the islands and gardens of the Hesperides, a sort of terrestrial paradise, appear to have been the Great West of the ancients, enveloped in mystery and poetry. Who has not seen in imagination, when looking into the sunset sky, the gardens of the Hesperides, and the foundation of all those fables?

If one is to use this passage he must have a control of it himself. If he does not understand the allusions to Lethe, Atlantis, and the gardens of the Hesperides, his dictionary will help him a good deal, the *Oxford Companion to Classical Literature* more. And he must try to see the implications of the metaphors. What does the extended metaphor of the compass needle suggest? What is implied in the last paragraph?

Now how is the passage to be used? It supplies no statistics, no particular historical fact except the apparently trivial one that Thoreau took a westerly direction in his daily walks. But it has a good deal to say about the impetus of the Westward movement. Here is an example of one way it might be used.

Henry David Thoreau, in an essay written late in his life, sees the Westward movement as "the prevailing tendency of my countrymen." Indeed, his own daily walk for exercise, which always took a westerly direction, becomes for him a tiny symbol of the impetus of his countrymen Westward, an impetus that was not just a desire for gain nor quite a reasoned thing: his comparisons are to the inevitable movement of a compass needle, and to the instinctive migration of birds and animals. "I must," he says, "walk toward Oregon, and not toward Europe. And that way the nation is moving." When Americans crossed the Atlantic, Thoreau thinks, they nearly forgot their European pasts, just as the shades in Virgil's Aeneid who drank of the river Lethe were prepared by the obliteration of their pasts to become new men. Yet there may be some ironic reservation in what Thoreau says of the Westward movement: he seems to ask us, did not the ancients think of their mythical great good places— Atlantis, the gardens of the Hesperides—as in the West, and may not the dreams of Americans be like the visions one sees in the sunset sky, of vapor only? Nevertheless, "we go westward as into the future," he says, "with a spirit of enterprise and adventure."16 He saw that for Americans, almost throughout the nineteenth century, the future had a geographical direction, that for them the future kept receding into the West.

16"Walking" (1862), reprinted in Writer to Reader, ed. Neal Frank Doubleday (Boston, 1966), pp. 38–39.

The discussion of the Thoreau passage makes rather a long paragraph, but in the assumed paper it would probably be well to hold this discussion together as a one-paragraph unit of the development (as was also done in the first use of the Crèvecoeur passage). The footnote is designed to indicate the nature of the source.

For any such interpretive account as this, the crucial question is whether or not the writer's intention in the use of his source will be clear to the reader who has not read the source. You may ask that question about the example above; and you should remember always to ask it about your own work. What the source paper writer writes has to stand on its own feet—he cannot assume his readers have read his sources.

7 problems in the combination of sources

This chapter will show how sources may be used together in various ways. It takes a little practice before one can manage such combinations easily. The intention here is to consider some typical problems and to suggest solutions.

The Proportional Use of Secondary Material

A recurrent tactical problem for student writers, as shown in Chapter 2, is likely to be the use of secondary material to supplement his primary material, while keeping the secondary material from usurping too much of his space. The following passage will provide a typical experiment.

From George Lyman Kittredge, *Witchcraft in Old and New England.* Cambridge, Mass.: Harvard University Press, 1929.

33   Further, our own attitude of mind toward witchcraft is a very modern attitude indeed. To us, one who asserts the existence, or even the possibility, of the crime of witchcraft staggers under a burden of proof which he cannot conceivably support. His thesis seems to us unreasonable, abnormal, monstrous; it can scarcely be stated in intelligible terms; it savors of madness. Now, before we can do any kind of justice to our forefathers,—a matter, be it remembered, of no moment to them, for they have gone to their reward, but, I take it, of considerable importance to us,—we must empty our heads of all such rationalistic ideas. To the contemporaries of William Stoughton and Samuel Sewall the existence of this crime was not merely an historical phenomenon, it was a fact of contemporary experience. Whoever denied the occurrence of witchcraft in the past, was an atheist; whoever refused to admit its actual possibility in the present, was either stubbornly incredulous, or destitute of the ability to draw an inference. Throughout the seventeenth century, very few persons could be found—not merely in New England, but in the whole world—who would have ventured to take so radical a position. That there had been witches and sorcerers in antiquity was beyond cavil. That there

were, or might be, witches and sorcerers in the present was almost equally certain. The crime was recognized by the Bible, by all branches of the Church, by philosophy, by natural science, by the medical faculty, by the law of England. I do not offer these postulates as novelties. They are commonplaces. They will not be attacked by anybody who has even a slight acquaintance with the mass of testimony that might be adduced to establish them.

The paragraph is beautifully developed, but the source paper writer who would use it must reduce it a good deal. He may try to see whether he can excise it enough so that he can quote it; but if he does, he will soon find that, even severely excised, it will make a quotation longer than is warranted in the use of a secondary source. If his purpose in restatement is fairly broad, he might produce the following and try to work it into a paper:

Although a belief in the actuality of witchcraft seems now impossible in any reasonable person, the Puritans, George Lyman Kittredge reminds us, lived in the seventeenth century. Then anyone who did not believe in the existence of witches in the past was considered an atheist, and anyone who denied the existence of witches in the present was considered to be willfully or stupidly denying experience. The crime of witchcraft, Kittredge says, was recognized by religious, scientific, and legal authority.

There might be a paper topic and purpose that would justify this restatement—perhaps a paper primarily concerned with the universality of the belief in witchcraft in the seventeenth century. (Notice that Kittredge's name is twice used in order to make clear that the whole passage is drawn from him.) But for most short papers and sharply defined purposes, a more economical and compact use is required. Just what can be compressed, reduced, or omitted will depend on how the passage will combine with other sources to serve the writer's topic and purpose.

It is important to remember that a writer uses his sources, primary as well as secondary, for his own purpose—that the fabric of the paper is his own. The example below will show how the Kittredge passage, combined with two other sources, one primary and one secondary, might fit into a paper concerned with understanding the Salem witchcraft trials of 1692.

Our difficulty in understanding the Salem trials is in realizing the assumptions under which they proceeded. The difficulty is the greater because, in most affairs of life, the citizens of Massachusetts in the late seventeenth century seem to us hard headed and perceptive. But to the modern mind, much of the testimony accepted at the witchcraft trials seems just absurd. The report of the examination of Mary Osgood, for example, records her testimony that when she first saw the devil, he was in the form of a cat; that she and three others "were carried upon a pole," through the air for some distance; that she "afflicted" by "pinching her bed clothes, and giving consent that the devil should do it in her shape, and that the devil could not do it without her consent."[5] One may wonder on what logic the court, which accepted this apparent nonsense as a confession, might suppose that a woman who had given her fealty to the devil could in any way restrict his actions.

Yet our thinking probably proceeds from the assumption that witchcraft is impossible. George Lyman Kittredge reminds us that throughout the seventeenth century the crime of witchcraft was recognized by all religious, scientific, and legal authority; and that its actuality in the past and possibility in the present were fully believed in by virtually all.[6] And as Charles Lamb asks, "When once . . . the lawless agency of bad spirits [was] assumed, what measures of probability . . . could [our forefathers] have to guide them in the rejection or admission of any particular testimony?"[7]

[5]Quoted in Thomas Hutchinson, The History of the Colony and Province of Massachusetts-Bay, ed. Lawrence Shaw Mayo (Cambridge, Mass., 1936), II, 24.
[6]Witchcraft in Old and New England (Cambridge, Mass., 1929), p. 330.
[7]"Witches, and Other Night Fears," The Essays of Elia (London: Oxford World's Classics, 1946), p. 94.

Notice the relationship between the two paragraphs: the first states and illustrates a problem; the second comments upon it. Notice, too, a couple of technical matters. For grammatical completeness a verb is inserted in brackets in the excised sentence from Lamb. The practice is sometimes a convenience, but it should be used sparingly, and one should not insert more than a word or two. The footnote for the Lamb sentence is designed to distinguish the edition clearly, for there are many editions of The Essays of Elia.

Making Purposeful Use of Scattered Sources

The source paper writer has to make the most he can from what he finds in his sources. Here is an instance in which he cannot find much, but in which he should not neglect the little that he finds. An example in Chapter 4 showed the structure of a paper on Cincinnati, Ohio, as it was seen by foreign observers in the second quarter of the nineteenth century. Using that same paper for the present example, assume that the writer has come to the third section of it, the cultural life of the new city. One evidence of that cultural life is what his sources have to say of museums. He finds these three short passages.

From Mrs. Frances Trollope, *Domestic Manners of the Americans.* 2 vols. London: Whittaker, Treacher & Co., 1832.

I,89   Cincinnati has not many lions to boast of, but among them / are two museums of natural history; both of these contain many respectable specimens, particularly

that of Mr. Dorfeuille, who has, moreover, some highly interesting Indian antiqui-
ties. He is a man of taste and science, but a collection formed strictly according
to their dictates, would by no means satisfy the western metropolis. The people
have a most extravagant passion for wax figures, and the two museums vie with
each other in displaying specimens of this barbarous branch of art. As Mr. Dorfeuille cannot trust to his science for attracting the citizens, he has put his inge-
nuity into requisition, and this has proved to him the surer aid of the two. He has
constructed a pandaemonium in an upper story of his museum, in which he has
congregated all the images of horror that his fertile fancy could devise; dwarfs
that by machinery grow into giants before the eyes of the spectator; imps of ebony
with eyes of flame; monstrous reptiles devouring youth and beauty; lakes of fire,
I,90 and mountains of ice; in / short, wax, paint, and springs have done wonders. "To
give the scheme some more effect," he makes it visible only through a grate of
massive iron bars, among which are arranged wires connected with an electrical
machine in a neighbouring chamber; should any daring hand or foot obtrude
itself within the bars, it receives a smart shock, that often passes through many
of the crowd, and the cause being unknown, the effect is exceedingly comic;
terror, astonishment, curiosity, all are set in action, and all contribute to make
"Dorfeuille's Hell" one of the most amusing exhibitions imaginable.

From Harriet Martineau, *Retrospect of Western Travel.* 2 vols. London:
Saunders and Otley, 1838.

II,   The greater part of the next morning was occupied with visitors; but we found
46 an interval to go out, under the guidance of friends, to see a few things which
lay near at hand. We visited the Museum, where we found, as in all new museums
whose rooms want filling up, some trumpery among much which is worthy to
remain. There was a mermaid not very cleverly constructed, and some bad wax
figures, posted like sentinels among the cases of geological and entomological
specimens; but, on the whole, the Museum is highly creditable to the zeal of its
contributors. There is, among other things, a pretty complete collection of the
currency of the country, from the earliest colonial days, and some of other countries with it. I hope this will be persevered in, and that the Cincinnati merchants
will make use of the opportunities afforded by their commerce of collecting specimens of every kind of currency used in the world, from the gilt and stamped leather
of the Chinese and Siberians to the last of Mr. Biddle's twenty-dollar notes. There
is a reasonable notion abroad that the Americans are the people who will bring
the philosophy and practice of exchanges to perfection; and theirs are the museums in which should be found a full history of currency, in the shape of a complete set of specimens.

From Charles Augustus Murray, *Travels in North America.* 2 vols. London:
Richard Bentley, 1839.

I,   The museum contains little worthy of notice; moreover, its contents, mean as they
203 are, are miserably deficient in order and arrangement. I was surprised and dis-
appointed, as I had heard much of the valuable collection to be seen in this estab-
lishment. There are a few fossil mammoth bones of extraordinary size, and also a
number of skulls found in some of the ancient mounds, differing materially in

I, form from those of the modern race of / Indians. There are also several banks and
204 insurance companies, and about twenty periodical publications, three or four of
which are daily papers; I also saw one German weekly paper, *Der Deutsche Frank-
lin,* as well written and better printed than most of those which I have seen in
the provincial towns in Germany.

Now these three pieces of source material, although they show something
of the cultural life of Cincinnati, do not warrant more than an economical
treatment in a single paragraph. But since they are scrappy and seem to include
some discrepancies in observation, combining them offers a little difficulty.
The obvious way of combining them would be to make successive summary
accounts of the three sources: "Mrs. Trollope says . . . . Miss Martineau says
. . . . But Murray says . . . ." Yet here the obvious way would not be the best
way; it would be very uneconomical, it would not allow the source paper
writer to use the material to his purpose, and it would put the burden of evalu-
ating the material on the reader—where it does not belong.

The writer needs to consider the three passages carefully: to see where they
coincide and where they show some discrepancy, and to see what inferences
arise from what is said in them. Then, following the principle that he uses his
sources for his own well-defined purpose, he may write something like this:

Our English travelers were also interested in Cincinnati's
museums—at least Mrs. Trollope writes of two, although Miss Martineau and Murray write as if there were only one. The collections
in the one or in both seem to have been of unequal value and sometimes in bad taste, as might be expected in so young a city. Mrs.
Trollope speaks of "many respectable specimens" and Miss Martineau
of "much which is worthy to remain," but both remark an American
taste for wax figures, apparently pretty appalling ones. Evidently
there were good collections of Indian material and of American currency. Even Murray, who thinks the museum "mean" and disorderly,
was interested in some fossil mammoth bones and some ancient Indian
skulls.[8] But one museum had a grotesque and, one gathers, childish
exhibit of animated figures called "Dorfeuille's Hell," in which
the proprietor, Mrs. Trollope tells us, had "congregated all the
images of horror that his fertile fancy could devise," and which
had a sort of electric fence to shock the unwary spectator. Mrs.
Trollope seems to have found the exhibit amusing. Dorfeuille's
museum was apparently a private enterprise, for Mrs. Trollope says
his "Hell" was designed to attract the citizens not much interested
in his serious exhibits.[9]

[8]Trollope, I, 89; Martineau, II, 46; Murray, I, 203–204.
[9]Trollope, I, 89–90.

A few remarks about the paragraph may be in point. Some students, whether
from over-conscientiousness or lack of clear purpose, may tend to include in

their papers almost anything that may be in the sources. In this case the writer has wisely passed over Miss Martineau's idea about the desirability of a currency collection, which is outside the specific concern of this paragraph.

With sources like these the writer is often forced to make some inferences. But it should always be made clear what is inference and what is restatement of source. You might consider the paragraph and see whether or not the distinction is always clear in it. Finally, in dealing with three or more sources in one paragraph, one may need to take a little trouble to avoid over-many footnotes. Notice in footnote 8 the combination of three references separated by semicolons; they would be quite sufficient to enable a reader to find the basis for the discussion in the sources.

Two Sources in Literary Discussion

In this section and in the next, the examples are intended to illustrate the discussion of related documents. The matter has been discussed in a general way in Chapter 4, where the concern was structural planning. There we considered the importance of making clear at the outset the nature of the documents and the purpose in dealing with them. Since we assume that the example passages in this and the next section come well along in their respective papers, we assume that the initial preparation for them has been done. But here is some indication of what it would have been for this first example:

The following example assumes a not-very-ambitious paper called "Poe as a Critic of Hawthorne." Edgar Allan Poe wrote two reviews of Nathaniel Hawthorne's work. The paper should consider the reviews in their relationship to the work by Hawthorne being reviewed. The example considers what Poe had to say on "The Minister's Black Veil" in his 1842 review of *Twice-Told Tales*. The structural plan is simple enough; the discussion proceeds from Poe's little critique of the tale to what basis there is for it in the tale. Everything Poe said of this tale is quoted in the example passage.

Perhaps the most interesting passage in Poe's 1842 review is his discussion of "The Minister's Black Veil." In it Poe begins a critical discussion of the tale that has continued to our time, and he seems to recognize the quality in Hawthorne's work that recent critics call his "ambiguity." Poe says of the tale:

> "The Minister's Black Veil" is a masterly composition, of which the sole defect is that to the rabble its exquisite skill will be <u>caviare</u>. The <u>obvious</u> meaning of this article will be found to smother its insinuated one. The <u>moral</u> put into the mouth of the dying minister will be supposed to convey the <u>true</u> import of the narrative; and that a crime of dark dye (having reference to the "young lady") has been committed, is a point which only minds congenial with that of the author will perceive.[6]

[6]Reprinted in <u>American Poetry and Prose</u>, ed. Norman Foerster (Boston, 1957), I, 398a.

What Poe calls "the <u>moral</u>" is clear enough: in the next-to-last paragraph of the tale the Reverend Mr. Hooper, on his death-bed, says that his parishioners have half recognized the veil as the symbol of the burden of concealment they, and all men, must carry.[7] The "young lady" to whom Poe refers is the young lady whose funeral Mr. Hooper so affectingly conducts during the first Sunday on which he wears the veil.

A passage in the account of the funeral seems to have suggested Poe's interpretation. As the minister bends over the coffin, he hastily pulls back his veil, as if he fears the corpse might see his face, and "a superstitious old woman" affirms that at this moment "the corpse had slightly shuddered" (pp. 57–58). Later as the mourners are leaving, a woman who has looked back at Mr. Hooper remarks, "I had a fancy that the minister and the maiden's spirit were walking hand in hand" (p. 58). But this remark, although it may suggest some connection between the minister and the young lady, hardly suggests "a crime of dark dye."

Possibly other passages support Poe's interpretation. The narrator of the story speaks of "an ambiguity of sin or sorrow, which enveloped the poor minister" (p. 65), and when his fiancée warns him that "there may be whispers that you hide your face under the consciousness of secret sin," Mr. Hooper answers, "If I hide my face for sorrow, there is cause enough; and if I cover it for secret sin, what mortal might not do the same?" (p. 62) The reader may wish, as Poe does not, to let this ambiguity stand unresolved. And he may ask why the account of the funeral has an authority in the interpretation of the tale that the dying words of Mr. Hooper do not.

[7]<u>Twice-Told Tales</u>, p. 69, in <u>Works</u>, Riverside Edition. Subsequent page references to <u>Twice-Told Tales</u> appear in the text.

Handling such material as this presents no great difficulty. In the example it was necessary only to relate the Poe passage to the tale in an orderly way. The first paragraph deals with the general reference Poe is making to the tale — the ambiguity of interpretation between the veil as a *symbol* of sin and as a *sign* of actual sin. The second paragraph describes the specific basis in the tale for Poe's interpretation; and the third considers further passages in the tale which may be supposed to support Poe's interpretation and which it is likely he had in mind. The last two sentences indicate the student writer's stand. The use of the present tense in the account of the tale is, as you doubtless recognize, a common convention in literary discussion.

The footnotes have been included for illustrative purposes. Notice in footnote 6 the page number; it designates a reference to the first column of a two-column page. The short form in 7 can be used since the Riverside Edition is well known and was for years the only standard edition of Hawthorne. But unless you are sure you are using a standard edition, use the form illustrated in Chapter 5. Possibly the parenthetical documentation is unnecessary. Since "The Minister's Black Veil" is short, the reader of the source paper could find, with a little trouble, the passages quoted or referred to.

A Study of the Composition of a Novel

A paper on the relationship of a literary work to its "raw material" presents special problems in economy. Here is an extended example.

When John William De Forest wrote his novel *Miss Ravenel's Conversion from Secession to Loyalty* (1867), he drew largely upon his record of his own experience in the War between the States, the record that is now printed as *A Volunteer's Adventures*. The two passages from the novel reprinted below have very close connections with the passages reprinted from *A Volunteer's Adventures*. Assume a paper to be called "Experience into Fiction: A Study of John William De Forest." Assume further that the background for the study has been presented—it has been pointed out, for example, that Captain Colburne, the hero of the novel, is stationed in the same places that De Forest was, and goes on the same campaigns that De Forest did, but that he is not a self-portrait on De Forest's part.

The difficulty in this project is largely technical and arises in the writing of the paper, not in seeing the relationship between the journal record and the novel—that is obvious enough. The problem is to discuss that relationship economically and in a way easy for the reader to follow. Here are the sources.

From John William De Forest, *Miss Ravenel's Conversion from Secession to Loyalty,* ed. Gordon S. Haight. New York: Rinehart & Co., 1955.

131 . . . The Langdons and Mrs. Larue proceeded to discuss affairs political, meta-
        phorically tying Beast Butler to a flaming stake and performing a scalp dance
        around it, making a drinking cup of his skull, quaffing from it refreshing draughts
        of Yankee blood. Lillie remembered that, disagreeably loyal as the New Boston
        ladies were, she had not heard from their lips any such conversational atrocities.
        She did not sympathize much when Mrs. Langdon entered on a lyrical recital of
        her own wrongs and sorrows. She was sorry, indeed, to hear that young Fred Lang-
132 don had been killed at Fort Jackson; but then / the mother expressed such a squaw-
        like fury for revenge as quite shocked and rather disgusted our heroine; and more-
        over she could not forget how coolly she had been treated merely because she
        was her dear father's daughter. She actually felt inclined to laugh satirically when
        the two visitors proceeded to relate jointly and with a species of solemn ferocity
        how they had that morning snubbed a Yankee officer.
           "The brute got up and offered us his seat in the cars. I didn't look at him. Neither
        of us looked at him. I said—we both said—'We accept nothing from Yankees.' I
        remained—we both remained—standing."
           Such was the mild substance of the narrative, but it was horrible in the telling,
        with fierce little hisses and glares, sticking out from it like quills of the fretful porcu-
        pine. Miss Ravenel did not sympathize with the conduct of the fair snubbers, and
        I fear also that she desired to make them feel uncomfortable.
           "Really," she observed, "I think it was right civil in him to give up his seat. I

didn't know that they were so polite. I thought they treated the citizens with all sorts of indignities."

To this the Langdons vouchsafed no reply except by rising and taking their departure.

. . . .

254 Colburne . . . is dark-red with sunburn; gaunt with bad food, irregular food, fasting, and severe marching; gaunt and wiry, but all the hardier and stronger for it, like a wolf. His coarse fatigue uniform is dirty with sleeping on the ground and with marching through mud and clouds of dust. It has been soaked over and over again with rain or perspiration, and then powdered thickly with the fine-grained, unctuous soil of Louisiana, until it is almost stiff enough to stand alone. He cannot wash it, because it is the only suit he has brought with him, and because moreover he never knows but that he may be ordered to fall in and march at five minutes' notice.

Yet his body and even his mind are in the soundest and most enviable health. His constant labors and hardships, and his occasional perils have preserved him from that enfeebling melancholy which often infects sensitive spirits upon whom has beaten a storm of trouble. Always in the open air, never poisoned by the neighborhood of four walls and a roof, he never catches cold, and rarely fails to have more appetite than food. He has borne as well as the hardiest mason or farmer

255 those / terrific forced marches which have brought the army from Camp Beasland to Alexandria on a hot scent after the flying and scattering Rebels. His feet have been as sore as any man's; they have been blistered from toe to heel, and swollen beyond their natural size; but he has never yet lain down by the roadside nor crawled into an army wagon, saying that he could march no further. He is loyal and manly in his endurance and is justly proud of it. In one of his letters he says, "I was fully repaid for yesterday's stretch of thirty-five miles by overhearing one of my Irishmen say, while washing his bloody feet, 'Be— —! but he's a hardy man, the Captin!' — To which another responded, 'An' he had his hands full to kape the byes' courage up; along in the afthernoon, he was a jokin' an' scoldin' an' encouragin' for ten miles together. Be— —! an' when *he* gives out, it 'ull be for good rayson.'" . . .

It was through an atmosphere of scalding heat and stifling dust that the brigade marched up the bluffs of Bayou Sara and over the rounded eminences which stretched on to Port Hudson. The perspiration which drenched the ragged uniforms

256 and the pulverous soil which powdered them rapidly mixed into a muddy / plaster; and the same plaster grimed the men's faces out of almost all semblance to humanity, except where the dust clung dry and gray to hair, beard, eyebrows, and eyelashes. So dense was the distressing cloud that it was impossible at times to see the length of a company. It seemed as if the men would go rabid with thirst, and drive the officers mad with their pleadings to leave the ranks for water, a privilege not allowable to any great extent in an enemy's country. A lovely crystal streamlet, running knee-deep over clean yellow sand, a charming contrast to black or brown bayous with muddy and treacherous banks, was forded by the feverish ranks with shouts and laughter of childlike enjoyment. But it was through volumes of burning yet lazy dust, soiling and darkening the glory of sunset, that the brigade reached its appointed bivouac in a large clearing, only two miles from the Rebel stronghold, though hidden from it by a dense forest of oaks, beeches, and magnolias.

From John William De Forest, *A Volunteer's Adventures,* ed. James H. Croushore. New Haven: Yale University Press, 1946.

51   I must tell you of an adventure of mine with one of the heroines of secession. On my way down to the city in the crowded, dirty cars, I saw behind me, standing, a lady in half-mourning, a pallid and meagre young woman, with compressed thin lips, sharp grey eyes and a waspish expression. Much doubting whether my civility would be well received, I rose and offered her my seat. She would not look at me; she just conceded me a quick shake of the head and a petulant shrug of the shoulders; then, pinching her pale lips, she stood glaring straight before her.

After waiting her pleasure a moment I resumed my seat. Presently a rather pretty lady opposite me (a young mother with kindly eyes and a cultured expression) took her little girl into her lap and beckoned the scowling heroine to the vacant place. She accepted it with lavish thanks, adding in a loud, ostentatious tone, "*I* wasn't going to take a seat from a Yankee. These cars used to be a fit place for ladies. Now niggers and Yankees crowd decent people out."

The lady with the kindly eyes threw me an apologetic glance which seemed to say, "I hope you did not hear." There ended the comedy; or was it a tragedy?
. . . .

92   Oh, the horrors of marching on blistered feet! It is an incessant bastinado applied by one's own self, from morning to night. I do not mean a single blister, as big as a pea, but a series of blisters, each as large as a dollar, or, to judge by one's sensations, as large as a cartwheel. I have had them one under the other, on the heel, on the ball of the foot, on every toe, a network, a labyrinth, an archipelago of agony. Heat, hunger, thirst, and fatigue are nothing compared with this torment. When you stand, you seem to be on red-hot iron plates; when you walk, you make grimaces at every step. In the morning the whole regiment starts limping, and by noon the best soldiers become nearly mutinous with suffering. They snarl and swear at each other; they curse the general for ordering such marching; they curse the enemy for running away instead of fighting; they fling themselves down in the dust, refusing to move a step further. Fevered with fatigue and pain, they are actually not themselves. Meantime, the company officers, as sore-footed as anyone, must run about from straggler to straggler, coaxing, arguing, ordering, and, perhaps, using the flat of the sabre. Instead of marching in front of my company,
93 I fol- / lowed immediately in the rear, so that I could see and at once pounce upon everyone who fell out.

It was curious to note how cheerful everyone became if cannon in front told of the proximity of the enemy. We were ready to fight the bloodiest of combats rather than march a mile further. We filed into line of battle delighted, and then resumed our pursuit heartsick.

It will be asked, perhaps, whether I, an officer and claiming, of course, to be a patriot, preserved my staunchness under these trials. I must confess, and I do it without great shame, conscious of being no more than human, that in my inmost soul I was as insubordinate as the worst men were in speech and behavior. In my unspeakable heart I groaned and raved. I wished the bridges would break down — I wished the regiment would refuse to take another step — it seemed to me that I should have been silent in the face of mutiny. But nothing of all this passed my lips, and none could suspect it from my actions.

When we bivouacked at night came the severest trial. Our regiment was on the left of the brigade, and as we always slept in line of battle, this threw us half a mile from the bayou, along which we marched, and which was our only source of water. It was necessary to order a squad of the blistered and bloody-footed men to bring water for the company's coffee. The first sergeant takes out his book and reads off the fatigue detail: "Corporal Smith, Privates Brown, Jones, Robinson, and Brown second, fall in with canteens to get water."

Now ensues a piteous groaning, pleading, and showing of bloody heels or blistered soles, on the part of the most fagged or least manly of the victims of rotation in labor. The first sergeant feels that he has no discretion in the matter, and he knows, moreover, that the other men are fully as incapable of marching as these. He stands firm on his detail, and the opposition grumblingly yields. Slowly and sadly Messrs. Brown, Jones, Robinson, and Brown second take up the canteens of the company, each backing six or eight, and limp away to the river, returning, an hour later, wet, muddy, dragged out, and savage.

Somewhat similar scenes happened on the march. Aides passed down the
94 length of the trailing column with the order, / "Water half a mile in front; details will be sent forward with canteens." Under these circumstances, roguish soldiers would sometimes use the chance to forage, falling in an hour later with a load of chickens as well as of fluid.

Having tried various alleviations for the hardships of marching, without much benefit, I conclude that man was not made to foot it at the rate of thirty miles a day. Soaping the inside of the stockings does some good, by diminishing the friction and, as a consequence, the blistering. It is also advisable to wash the feet before starting, always providing you have sufficient time and water. Beware of washing them at night; it cracks the heated skin and increases the misery. Beware, too, of trying to march on the strength of whiskey; you go better for a few minutes, and then you are worse off than ever. Opium is far superior as a temporary tonic, if I may judge by a single day's experience. I started out sick, took four grains of opium, marched better and better every hour, and at the end of twenty-two miles came in as fresh as a lark.

It must be understood by the non-military reader that company officers of infantry are not permitted to mount horses, whether by borrowing or stealing, but must foot it alongside of their men, for the double purpose of keeping them in order and of setting them an example of hardihood. On this march, General Banks impounded, at a certain point on the road, more than a dozen infantry officers who were found astride of animals, causing each to rejoin his command as it passed, placing some under arrest and summarily dismissing one from the service. They looked exceedingly crestfallen as they stood there, cooped up in a barnyard under charge of the provost guard. The passing soldiers grinned at them, hooted a little, and marched on, much cheered by the spectacle.

If it had not been for the counter irritant of blistered feet, we should have heard a mutinous deal of grumbling on account of thirst. A man strapped up as a soldier is, and weighted with forty rounds of ammunition, knapsack, three days' rations, canteen containing three pints, and rifle, perspires profusely. I have seen the sweat standing on the woolly fibres of their flannel sacks like dew. To supply this waste of moisture they pour down the warm water of their canteens, and are soon beg-
95 ging / for leave to fall out of the ranks in search of incredibly situated springs and rivulets. It will not do to accede to the request, for if one man goes, all have a right to go, and, moreover, the absence would probably terminate in a course of forag-

ing or pillaging. Mindful of his duty and the orders of his superiors, the captain grimly responds, "Keep your place, sir," and trudges sufferingly on, cursing inwardly the heat, the dust, the pace and, perhaps, the orders. He knows that if his fellows are caught a mile to the rear wringing the necks of chickens, he may be sent after them; and, in view of his blisters and the fifteen miles already marched and the indefinite miles yet to go, he has no fancy for such an expedition. . . .

In describing the miseries of marching, I must not forget the dust. The movement of so many thousands of feet throws up such dense and prodigious clouds that one who has not witnessed the phenomenon will find it difficult to imagine it in all its vastness and nuisance. The officers dodge from side to side of the road to escape the pulverous suffocation; and the men, bound to their fours, choke desperately along in the midst of it. The faces become grimed out of all human semblance; the eyelashes are loaded, the hair discolored, and the uniform turns to the color of the earth. It frequently happens that you cannot see the length of your regiment, and it has occurred to me that I have been unable to see the length of 96 my own company of per- / haps twenty files. Of course, this annoyance varies greatly in magnitude, according to the nature of the earth.

First consider the second passage from *Miss Ravenel's Conversion* (it is from Chapter XX). As you have seen, it uses a good many details from *A Volunteer's Adventures*. How will the source paper writer make clear the relationship of the passage from the novel to the journal record? One possibility is a two-paragraph discussion, the first paragraph concerned with the passage from the novel, the second with the source material for it in the journal. Such a discussion is feasible; indeed it might work well if the order of detail were kept exactly parallel in the two paragraphs. For example if the first detail in the first paragraph were the matter of blisters, that matter should be the first detail in the second. Yet at best that organization would put much of the burden of comparison on the reader. But try it another way. It is not at all necessary that every resemblance between the novel and the journal record be pointed out; what is wanted is clear and adequate illustration. The first short paragraph in the example below would be a major transition in the paper.

But these general relationships do not show the intimate connection between A Volunteer's Adventures and Miss Ravenel's Conversion. To realize that, one must examine particular passages in the novel against their sources in De Forest's account of his war experience.

Some of De Forest's experiences are given to Captain Colburne in Chapter XX of Miss Ravenel's Conversion. In A Volunteer's Adventures De Forest records the misery of blisters: "I have had them," he says, "one under the other, on the heel, behind the heel, on the ball of the foot, on every toe, a network, a labyrinth, an archipelago of agony."[1] Captain Colburne has the same sort of blisters, much less extravagantly described: "His feet have been as sore as any man's; they have been blistered from toe to heel, and swollen beyond their natural size."[2] Again in his journal account De Forest remarks the necessity of an officer keeping a semblance

of cheerfulness and courage: "In my inmost soul," he says, "I was
as insubordinate as the worst men were in speech and behavior. . . .
But nothing of all this passed my lips, and none could suspect it
from my actions" (p. 93). In the novel De Forest is free to exalt
his hero: Captain Colburne "has never yet lain down by the roadside nor crawled into an army wagon, saying that he could march no
further. He is loyal and manly in his endurance and is justly proud
of it" (p. 255). Although some expressions in the journal and in
the novel are closely parallel, De Forest seems always to make at
least a slight revision. For example, in the journal record, the
faces of the men marching in the dust "become grimed out of all human semblance" (p. 95); in the novel, a plaster of perspiration and
dust "grimed the men's faces out of almost all semblance to humanity" (p. 256). De Forest often writes with his eye on his journal,
but he is writing a new work.

[1]A Volunteer's Adventures, ed. by James H. Croushore (New
Haven, 1946), p. 92. Subsequent page references to A Volunteer's
Adventures appear in the text.
[2]Miss Ravenel's Conversion from Secession to Loyalty, ed. by
Gordon S. Haight (New York, 1955), p. 255. Subsequent page refer-
ences to Miss Ravenel's Conversion appear in the text.

Short paragraphs, like the one that begins this example, are an excellent
means to make major transitions, but not minor ones — lest the paragraphing
become scrappy and confusing. In the comparisons made in the second paragraph, notice the expressions intended to show the reader what are the like-
nesses and differences in the pair of passages.

When page references to two books are made parenthetically, one needs
to take particular care that the text makes clear what book is referred to in
each instance. In the footnotes that prepare for the parenthetical documentation, the use of the titles of both books, even though both titles appear in the
text, prevents a possible confusion when two such footnotes appear together.
The short title *Miss Ravenel's Conversion* may be used continually in the text
after the full title has been used at the first reference to the book.

Adjusting Differences in Narrative Point of View. In the example above,
the source paper writer worked with a portion of *Miss Ravenel's Conversion*
in which De Forest merely made his own military experience into that of his
hero, Captain Colburne. The difference between the journal and the novel in
narrative point of view gave the source paper writer no difficulty. But in handling the two accounts of the horse car incident, the difference in narrative
point of view does make a difficulty. The problem will be to make the relationship of the two accounts clear without using too much space in explanation.
Here is one way to solve that problem:

De Forest most often uses his experience by transposing it to
his account of Captain Colburne's activities; but he does find

ways of using it when Colburne is not at all involved in the narrative. One example will serve us. In A Volunteer's Adventures De Forest tells how he was thoroughly snubbed when, in a horse car, he tried to offer his seat to a Southern woman in half mourning (p. 51). In the novel what is essentially the same incident is related from quite a different point of view by a Mrs. Langdon—who has recently lost a son in battle—and her daughter. The two women, who are calling on Lillie Ravenel, feel that they have put a Yankee officer, unknown to them, in his place. They speak jointly: "The brute got up and offered us his seat in the cars. I didn't look at him. Neither of us looked at him. I said—we both said—'We accept nothing from Yankees.' I remained—we both remained—standing" (p. 132). In his journal account De Forest wondered if the incident were a comedy or a tragedy. In the novel it is treated as a comedy with disturbing overtones; but in both journal and novel it represents the implacable hatred of the woman of New Orleans for the occupying forces of the North. The Langdons have somewhat more refinement than the woman De Forest encountered, yet they relate their triumph with "fierce little hisses and glares."

The question to ask about this account is not whether it is clear to you — you have read the sources. Ask, rather, would it be clear to a reader of the source paper who had read neither of the sources.

8 the detail of structure

The principles of structure in writing the source paper are the principles of structure in composition in general. But sometimes students, distracted by the unfamiliar problems of handling sources, forget these familiar principles, or fail to see how they apply to new problems. The intention of this chapter is not to repeat instruction you have already had, but to supplement it by considering the application of quite ordinary principles of structure to the particular problems of the source paper.

Title and Beginning

Source paper titles commonly are longer than the titles of magazine articles, for the title of a source paper should be definitive. The title and the first few sentences of the paper should define the scope and purpose of the paper. You will do well to consider them as one problem; together they make a sort of contract with your reader. A title—no matter how clever—or an opening sentence—no matter how striking—that obscures or distracts from your topic or purpose will tend to defeat you.

That is not say you need be dull or mechanical. The most effective start, however, is one that gets your purpose stated and your procedure indicated, and goes at once into the discussion.

To experiment with some beginnings for a short paper, assume a paper concerned with Mark Twain's oral tales and the influence upon them of his friend Jim Gillis. One way of beginning would be to define the subject and predict the two-part structure to be used:

During Mark Twain's years in Nevada and California he had for a close friend Jim Gillis, pocket miner and accomplished story-teller. It is the intention of this paper to study, first, the personal relationships of the two, and then the influence of Gillis upon Twain's technique in the oral tale adapted for the printed page.

A second way of beginning is to use a quotation from Twain as a point
of departure:

In his "How to Tell a Story" Mark Twain remarks that he had been
"almost daily in the company of the most expert story-tellers for
many years." Of these experts, Twain's friend Jim Gillis was perhaps the most remarkable: he was, Twain says, "born a humorist and
a very competent one."

A third way is to use the reader's presumed acquaintance with the subject
as a point of departure:

Most readers of Mark Twain know his "Baker's Bluejay Yarn," the
amusing tale of a bluejay who tried to fill a house with acorns.
They will remember that, in introducing the story into A Tramp
Abroad, Twain ascribes it to one Jim Baker. This Jim Baker was
based upon a character invented by Twain's friend Jim Gillis, a
pocket miner in California.

All three examples make a sort of contract with the reader, the first most
obviously. As they are set down here, they may seem equally useful. But a
writer might find that one would suit his purpose and planned procedure much
better than either of the other two.

These examples will also illustrate the problem of the relationship between
title and beginning sentences. For the first example, the title "Jim Gillis and
Mark Twain" would do well enough. But the other two beginnings only imply
the paper's concern with the literary influence of Gillis on Twain; with them
the title should be something like "Jim Gillis' Influence on Mark Twain's Oral
Stories," or "Mark Twain, Jim Gillis, and the Frontier Oral Tale."

But you may be better able to see in the consideration of a long paper the
advantages of a clear and careful beginning that leads into a planned structure.
For example, assume that a student in an honor's course is to write on the
demand for a national literature in the United States between 1815 and 1835
as it applied to fiction. He is to work with primary sources — material written
within those years. He must deal, then, with the concept "literary nationalism"
as it is embodied in a number of documents. Even though his subject is properly
limited, his material is extensive and diverse. And he rather dreads writing a
paper of the considerable length his instructor asks.

The student is wise enough to spend sufficient time in considering just
how his material will best divide, and he finds that it makes for a three-part
treatment. After he has blocked out his paper he puts his signpost paragraph
into final form. He knows that his signpost should first of all define his subject
and intention, and then make clear the order of treatment. His signpost turns
out to be this:

In the first part of our literary history, literary discussion
was primarily concerned with the necessity of a peculiarly American literature. The discussion of literary nationalism in its re-

lation to fiction was indeed a dispute, for some writers asserted that American materials were insufficient or inappropriate for fictional use, and others that it was both a duty and privilege to use them. The present purpose is to study this discussion between 1815 and 1835 as it appears in critical articles in magazines, in addresses and orations, and in the statements of intent on the part of the fiction writers themselves.

The signpost listing at the end of this signpost paragraph will make transition between sections of the paper easy. The sections begin thus:

i

From its founding in 1815, the <u>North American Review</u> carried articles in which . . .

ii

The demand for a national literature was not only a subject for magazine articles. It was also a favorite subject for public speakers, who . . .

iii

Although critics and orators shaped the theory of literary nationalism, practicing fiction writers joined the discussion, and their statements of intention . . .

Now what has been accomplished? The student has started at once, without the purposeless "introduction" that disfigures so many source papers. The first sentence in his signpost paragraph announces the field of inquiry. The second sentence develops the first. The third sentence announces the topic, establishes the order of discussion, and provides for between-section transition. Above all, the student has planned a structure he can handle. His three-part structure relieves him from attempting a complex and extended single structure. He can, instead, devise a structure for each section, although he will try to keep the sections as closely parallel in structure as the material allows. But he will be working with units of writing short enough to feel comfortable with.

Besides the signpost, one may need to make early in the paper another provision for subsequent discussion. A writer should consider what the reader needs to know first; if that is forgotten, some later discussion may have to be awkwardly interrupted with explanation.

Transition

You have long known about within-paragraph and between-paragraph transition, and the principles you have learned certainly apply to source paper writing. What bothers some students in source paper writing is distinguishing the transition that marks off sections or large units from the transition used between one paragraph and another closely connected with it.

Reconsider the example above, showing the beginnings of the three sections of the paper in literary nationalism. Notice the transitions between i and ii and between ii and iii. For lack of a better term, such a transition may be called a "heavy transition." In each instance, the first part of the transition looks back at what has been said, and the second part looks forward to the new discussion. (In the transition between i and ii, it is the first sentence that looks back; in the transition between ii and iii, the first clause looks back.) That is one way — a convenient way — to mark out an important transition. The beginnings of the sections would have been clearly indicated without the section numbers, which are, indeed, only a detail of external form, and do not lessen the necessity of clear transition between sections.

Such "heavy" transitions serve to mark out the divisions of the paper and to move the discussion along at the same time. But there are other ways of making marked transitions. Here is an example of a transition split between the end of one paragraph and the beginning of another.

The lack of international copyright was an advantage to American publishers, but a decided handicap to American authors.

The publishers enjoyed the opportunity of reprinting English work without paying royalty, and they were understandably reluctant to pay royalties for fiction written in America.

But of course the most decisive sort of transition is accomplished by a short paragraph given entirely to the transition.

Here are examples of transitional paragraphs. This one might appear in the paper about Hamlin Garland's life and works that was discussed in the last section of Chapter 4.

"The Return of a Private," then, reaches back into Garland's earliest memories, and has a clear relationship to the Garland family history. But the relationship of "Under the Lion's Paw" to Garland's experience and observation is a little more difficult to define, since for this story we have to consider also the influence of the teachings of Henry George's Progress and Poverty, 1879.

And this paragraph devoted entirely to transition might appear in the paper on Mark Twain and Jim Gillis.

"Baker's Bluejay Yarn" and the story of Tom Quartz are not only told in Gillis' manner; they were his stories to begin with. Twain's best known oral tale, "The Celebrated Jumping Frog," did not originate with Gillis, but he contributed something—perhaps a great deal—to Twain's development of it.

You will of course make your transitions by whatever means work best at the points they come. But do remember that the connections or the distinctions that are so clear in your mind will not be clear to your reader unless you state them for him.

Paragraphing and Paragraphs in Sequence

Chapters 6 and 7 were concerned with the handling of sources, but they were also concerned with the problem of paragraphing in the particular shape it takes in the source paper. Handling and combining sources are new difficulties, and students who in other sorts of writing manage their paragraphs well enough often fail to make their paragraphs clear units of discussion in their source papers. Sometimes even within a single paragraph a student allows himself to be controlled by his sources instead of using them for his purpose. Your instructor probably remembers with an amused horror paragraphs written after this pattern: "Jason Verbose states . . . . He also says . . . . Verbose further states . . . ." But avoiding this fault is only a matter of being aware of what one is doing.

What may be difficult is maintaining a pattern of several paragraphs. In it you need to remember that paragraphing is for the reader's convenience, to help *him* realize the relationships of fact and ideas. Therefore, if you have a plan clear enough so that you could, if asked, say how it will help your reader, your paragraphing is likely to be efficient. The matter is as simple — or as difficult — as that.

The structure of a paper, which paragraphing reflects, is often complicated by problems of how to discuss related documents. Such problems consistently involve ordering a discussion so that a reader can follow it, but individual problems must be resolved in somewhat different ways. Yet experience does suggest a principle of a sort: an efficient discussion of two documents together tends to have a structure that is implicit in the documents themselves, and this will be found in a careful examination of those documents. Perhaps the most obvious example is the discussion in Chapter 2 of a passage from a Jefferson letter and a passage from his *Notes on the State of Virginia*. But the structure used, although implicit in the relationship of the sources, must still be accommodated to a reader who knows those sources only through the paper he is reading.

Concluding

As some students have the notion that a source paper ought to have an introduction, so some may have the notion that it ought to have a section called a conclusion, which they may think of as a repetitious summary of what had been said in the paper. (The formal summary in some scientific papers is not appropriate to a general research or source paper.) The thing to avoid above all is writing a conclusion that will seem to the reader something tacked onto the paper after it should have ended.

A source paper does conclude in the sense that it comes to an end; and many source papers come to a conclusion, in the sense that they end with a judgment or a decision based on the evidence the paper has presented. Your conclusion should be what arises naturally and inevitably from your discussion. A writer may find difficulty, of course, in phrasing his conclusion to his satisfaction; but if he is in doubt about what he wants to say in it, his doubt suggests that his trouble goes far back into his planning of the paper.

The end position—in paragraph, section, or source paper—is always important, for it is your last chance at the reader in that unit. You will want to make the most of it in the source paper, and to use it for the idea, the discovery, the relationship, even the image that you wish to have stick in your reader's mind. If, for instance, in the paper on Jim Gillis and Mark Twain, the writer were most concerned to have his reader realize Twain's faculty for admiration and generous recognition of his own indebtedness, he would remark on that faculty at the close, even though he had given it attention in the foregoing discussion. If, on the other hand, the writer were primarily concerned with the oral tradition behind Twain's work, he would close on that concern. And so with more complex matters—the conclusion arises from the discussion and points up its purpose. The last rounding-off sentence may prove a very troublesome one; or it may come as if by inspiration.

Revision

The final revision, as you know, ought to be a process quite separate from the writing; it is best accomplished when a considerable time has elapsed since the writing of the paper, so that you can see what you have written as your reader will. Even as little as a full day between writing and revision is an advantage.

Now you cannot expect, of course, to do much to improve the large structure of your paper at the time of revision; you can hardly rework the whole— that is one reason why it has been insisted that the initial planning be careful and deliberate. And in revision you will be concerned to check your references and quotations, and to watch matters of spelling, punctuation and the like. But revision can include and ought to include attention to the detail of structure.

In particular, the process of revision is your second chance at paragraphing. It is not too late in revision to change the order of paragraphs, or to make one out of two, or two out of one. Try hard to put yourself in the position of your reader and to decide whether or not the paragraphing is serving him. And in revision, if it is a little removed in time from the writing, you are likely to be aware of your transition or the lack of it.

You had better give your paper one or two readings which concentrate on paragraphing and transition alone. Indeed, it is always well to use separate readings in which you concentrate on particular matters. Most persons—even practiced writers—cannot think about the accuracy of references and quotations, their weaknesses in spelling and punctuation, the structure and sequence of paragraphs, and the adequacy of transition all at the same time.

If you are wise enough and self-disciplined enough to plan your work so that you can really make revision a separate process, removed in time from the writing, it is safe to promise you this much: you will find that you can see your paper in perspective and as a whole, and you will be able to take care of those things you were doubtful about more easily than you expected.

9 a complete paper

In this chapter we have first an account of the inception of a source paper and a reprinting of its primary sources. Then the paper is reproduced. Finally there are some comments on the problems encountered in writing the paper. We shall assume that the paper is a student paper, and that we can follow the writer at any point in his procedure.

The Topic, the Determination of Sources, and the Planning

The paper is called "Packet Boat Travel on American Canals." The title is definitive enough, since passenger travel on American canals flourished only in the first half of the nineteenth century. The topic is not earth-shaking, but it can be handled in a relatively short paper; indeed 2500–3000 words are perhaps about what it is worth.

The subject emerged for the student in this fashion: some years before he entered college, he had read and enjoyed Samuel Hopkins Adams' *Grandfather Stories* (1955) and his *The Erie Canal* (1953), a reliable book designed for young readers. After the student knew he was to write a source paper, but for quite another assignment, he had read Nathaniel Hawthorne's story "Young Goodman Brown" in *Mosses from an Old Manse,* and he had noticed in that volume Hawthorne's account of a journey on a packet boat, a sketch called "The Canal Boat." He read it and found it interesting. At about the same time he noticed on the library's shelf of new acquisitions Ronald E. Shaw's *Erie Water West: A History of the Erie Canal 1792–1854* (1966). He thought it a good book, and he found that it had an extensive "Essay on Bibliography."

This coming together of a primary and a secondary source was fortuitous, but it is the sort of thing that is likely to happen when one has an interest in a subject to start with. Yet almost at once the student ran into a little difficulty. Although the bibliography in Shaw lists a number of primary sources having to do with packet boat travel, the most promising were unavailable. For instance, he found Shaw's quotation from Harriet Martineau's *Retrospect of Western Travel* (1838) interesting, and he found that his library did not have the book. (The student writer, even if he is using a large library, must always be braced for the difficulty of an unavailable source.) Moreover, as the student considered his Hawthorne source, he thought that it ought to be balanced by another account by a literary man known to his readers. One of the things he had learned from Shaw's bibliography was that a good many of the accounts of canal travel were written by foreign visitors.

The student tried Gohdes' *Bibliographical Guide*; it yielded him nothing directly but it did suggest to him that he might try the bibliographical volume of the *Literary History of the United States*. There he located in the index the entry "foreign observers," and within that entry he learned that Charles Dickens wrote a travel book, *American Notes for General Circulation* (1842). A glance at the table of contents of that book showed him that it included an account of a packet boat journey from Harrisburg, Pennsylvania, to Pittsburg. Now the student had been thinking only of packet boats on the Erie Canal, but he saw that he need merely change his focus a little in order to use the Dickens source. He was pleased to find that in some ways the accounts by Hawthorne and by Dickens are parallel. Then the student picked up one more primary source. His instructor remarked that he remembered some canal material in William Dean Howells' *A Boy's Town* (1890). The student found the passages, and thought them useful.

The bibliography in Shaw's *Erie Water West* led the student to a number of secondary sources; indeed one of them, Alvin F. Harlow's *Old Towpaths* (1926), proved to be more useful to his purpose than the Shaw volume itself. (He discovered that Harlow's book would have led him eventually to Dickens' account; still he thought he had done well to establish his primary sources at once.) The documentation of the paper will show most of the books the student consulted, but not all. Of course it will not show the two bibliographical works mentioned above. But it also will not show, for instance, that the student consulted Nina E. Browne's *A Bibliography of Nathaniel Hawthorne* to learn the place and date of the first printing of "The Canal Boat," or that he used the *Oxford Companion to American Literature* to learn when Dickens made his American journey (surprisingly in the same year his account of it was published).

The student found that the concentration in his paper and the division of his material were both pretty well governed by the nature of his primary sources. Since they are written from the viewpoints of passengers, his paper would not be much concerned with the technical side of canal boat operation nor its economics, even though his secondary sources have plenty of material on these matters.

At first the student thought of discussing the accounts by Hawthorne and by Dickens together, and of using this division: the design and operation of canal packet boats, their accommodations for passengers, and life on the canal and canalside. But he discarded the plan because it seemed not to allow him a way of giving his readers any realization of what a whole journey was like. He adopted instead the rather obvious plan of letting the separate discussion of his two major sources determine the sections of his paper. He thought his readers would be interested in the famous writers of his major sources in themselves, quite apart from their material, and this was a further justification for his plan.

The Primary Sources

Here are reprinted the primary sources for the paper. You can see what the writer has done with his sources—what he has selected and what he has omitted—only by comparing the sources and the paper. (In the selection from *A Boy's Town,* "my boy" is Howells' way of designating himself as a boy.)

From Nathaniel Hawthorne, "Sketches from Memory: The Canal Boat," *Mosses from an Old Manse, The Complete Works of Nathaniel Hawthorne,* II, ed. G. P. Lathrop: The Riverside Edition, 12 vols. Boston: Houghton, Mifflin and Company, 1883.

484   I was inclined to be poetical about the Grand Canal. In my imagination De Witt Clinton was an enchanter, who had waved his magic wand from the Hudson to Lake Erie and united them by a watery highway, crowded with the commerce of two worlds, till then inaccessible to each other. This simple and mighty conception had conferred inestimable value on spots which Nature seemed to have thrown carelessly into the great body of the earth, without foreseeing that they could ever attain importance. I pictured the surprise of the sleepy Dutchmen when the new river first glittered by their doors, bringing them hard cash or foreign commodities in exchange for their hitherto unmarketable produce. Surely the water
485 of this canal must be the most fertilizing of all fluids; for it causes towns, with / their masses of brick and stone, their churches and theatres, their business and hubbub, their luxury and refinement, their gay dames and polished citizens, to spring up, till in time the wondrous stream may flow between two continuous lines of buildings, through one thronged street, from Buffalo to Albany. I embarked about thirty miles below Utica, determining to voyage along the whole extent of the canal at least twice in the course of the summer.

Behold us, then, fairly afloat, with three horses harnessed to our vessel, like the steeds of Neptune to a huge scallop shell in mythological pictures. Bound to a distant port, we had neither chart nor compass, nor cared about the wind, nor felt the heaving of a billow, nor dreaded shipwreck, however fierce the tempest, in our adventurous navigation of an interminable mud puddle; for a mud puddle it seemed, and as dark and turbid as if every kennel in the land paid contribution to it. With an imperceptible current, it holds its drowsy way through all the dismal swamps and unimpressive scenery that could be found between the great lakes and the seacoast. Yet there is variety enough, both on the surface of the canal and along its banks, to amuse the traveller, if an overpowering tedium did not deaden his perceptions.

Sometimes we met a black and rustylooking vessel, laden with lumber, salt from Syracuse, or Genesee flour, and shaped at both ends like a square-toed boot, as if it had two sterns, and were fated always to advance backward. On its deck would be a square hut, and a woman seen through the window at her household work, with a little tribe of children, who perhaps had been born in this strange
486 dwelling and knew no other home. Thus, while the husband smoked his pipe / at the helm, and the eldest son rode one of the horses, on went the family, travelling hundreds of miles in their own house and carrying their fireside with them. The most frequent species of craft were the "line boats," which had a cabin at each end, and a great bulk of barrels, bales, and boxes in the midst, or light packets, like our own, decked all over with a row of curtained windows from stem to stern,

and a drowsy face at every one. Once we encountered a boat of rude construction, painted all in gloomy black, and manned by three Indians, who gazed at us in silence and with a singular fixedness of eye. Perhaps these three alone, among the ancient possessors of the land, had attempted to derive benefit from the white man's mighty projects and float along the current of his enterprise. Not long after, in the midst of a swamp and beneath a clouded sky, we overtook a vessel that seemed full of mirth and sunshine. It contained a little colony of Swiss on their way to Michigan, clad in garments of strange fashion and gay colors, scarlet, yellow, and bright blue, singing, laughing, and making merry in odd tones and a babble of outlandish words. One pretty damsel, with a beautiful pair of naked white arms, addressed a mirthful remark to me. She spoke in her native tongue, and I retorted in good English, both of us laughing heartily at each other's unintelligible wit. I cannot describe how pleasantly this incident affected me. These honest Swiss were an itinerant community of jest and fun journeying through a gloomy land and among a dull race of money-getting drudges, meeting none to understand their mirth, and only one to sympathize with it, yet still retaining the happy lightness of their own spirit.

487   Had I been on my feet at the time instead of sailing / slowly along in a dirty canal boat, I should often have paused to contemplate the diversified panorama along the banks of the canal. Sometimes the scene was a forest, dark, dense, and impervious, breaking away occasionally and receding from a lonely tract, covered with dismal black stumps where, on the verge of the canal, might be seen a log cottage and a sallow-faced woman at the window. Lean and aguish, she looked like poverty personified, half-clothed, half-fed, and dwelling in a desert, while a tide of wealth was sweeping by her door. Two or three miles farther would bring us to a lock, where the slight impediment to navigation had created a little mart of trade. Here would be found commodities of all sorts, enumerated in yellow letters on the window shutters of a small grocery store, the owner of which had set his soul to the gathering of coppers and small change, buying and selling through the week, and counting his gains on the blessed Sabbath. The next scene might be the dwelling-houses and stores of a thriving village, built of wood or small gray stones, a church spire rising in the midst, and generally two taverns, bearing over their piazzas the pompous titles of "hotel," "exchange," "tontine," or "coffee-house." Passing on, we glide now into the unquiet heart of an inland city,—of Utica, for instance,—and find ourselves amid piles of brick, crowded docks and quays, rich warehouses, and a busy population. We feel the eager and hurrying spirit of the place, like a stream and eddy whirling us along with it. Through the thickest of the tumult goes the canal, flowing between lofty rows of buildings and arched bridges of hewn stone. Onward, also, go we, till the hum and bustle of struggling enterprise die away behind us and we are threading an avenue of the ancient woods again.

488   This sounds not amiss in description, but was so tiresome in reality that we were driven to the most childish expedients for amusement. An English traveller paraded the deck, with a rifle in his walking stick, and waged war on squirrels and woodpeckers, sometimes sending an unsuccessful bullet among flocks of tame ducks and geese which abound in the dirty water of the canal. I, also, pelted these foolish birds with apples, and smiled at the ridiculous earnestness of their scrambles for the prize while the apple bobbed about like a thing of life. Several little accidents afforded us good-natured diversion. At the moment of changing horses the tow-

rope caught a Massachusetts farmer by the leg and threw him down in a very indescribable posture, leaving a purple mark around his sturdy limb. A new passenger fell flat on his back in attempting to step on deck as the boat emerged from under a bridge. Another, in his Sunday clothes, as good luck would have it, being told to leap aboard from the bank, forthwith plunged up to his third waistcoat button in the canal, and was fished out in a very pitiable plight, not at all amended by our three rounds of applause. Anon a Virginia schoolmaster, too intent on a pocket Virgil to heed the helmsman's warning, "Bridge! bridge!" was saluted by the said bridge on his knowledge box. I had prostrated myself like a pagan before his idol, but heard the dull, leaden sound of the contact, and fully expected to see the treasures of the poor man's cranium scattered about the deck. However, as there was no harm done, except a large bump on the head, and probably a corresponding dent in the bridge, the rest of us exchanged glances and laughed quietly. Oh, how pitiless are idle people! . . .

489   The table being now lengthened through the cabin and spread for supper, the next twenty minutes were the pleasantest I had spent on the canal, the same space at dinner excepted. At the close of the meal it had become dusky enough for lamplight. The rain pattered unceasingly on the deck, and sometimes came with a sullen rush against the windows, driven by the wind as it stirred through an opening of the forest. The intolerable dulness of the scene engendered an evil spirit in me. Perceiving that the Englishman was taking notes in a memorandum book, with occasional glances round the cabin, I presumed that we were all to figure in a future volume of travels, and amused my ill humor by falling into the probable vein of his remarks. He would hold up an imaginary mirror, wherein our reflected faces would appear ugly and ridiculous, yet still retain an undeniable likeness to the originals. Then, with more sweeping malice, he would make these caricatures the representatives of great classes of my countrymen.

He glanced at the Virginia schoolmaster, a Yankee by birth, who, to recreate himself, was examining a freshman from Schenectady College in the conjugation of a Greek verb. Him the Englishman would portray as the scholar of America, and compare his erudition to a schoolboy's Latin theme made up of scraps ill selected and worse put together. Next the tourist looked at the Massachusetts farmer, who was delivering a dogmatic harangue on the iniquity of Sunday mails. Here was the far-famed yeoman of New England; his religion, writes the Englishman, is gloom on the Sabbath, long prayers every morning and eventide, and illiberality at all times; his boasted information is merely an abstract and compound

490 of newspaper para- / graphs, Congress debates, caucus harangues, and the argument and judge's charge in his own lawsuits. The bookmonger cast his eye at a Detroit merchant, and began scribbling faster than ever. In this sharp-eyed man, this lean man, of wrinkled brow, we see daring enterprise and close-fisted avarice combined. Here is the worshipper of Mammon at noonday; here is the three times bankrupt, richer after every ruin; here, in one word, (O wicked Englishman to say it!) here is the American. He lifted his eye-glass to inspect a western lady, who at once became aware of the glance, reddened, and retired deeper into the female part of the cabin. Here was the pure, modest, sensitive, and shrinking woman of America,—shrinking when no evil is intended, and sensitive like diseased flesh, that thrills if you but point at it; and strangely modest, without confidence in the modesty of other people; and admirably pure, with such a quick apprehension of all impurity.

In this manner I went all through the cabin, hitting everybody as hard a lash as I could, and laying the whole blame on the infernal Englishman. At length I caught the eyes of my own image in the looking-glass, where a number of the party were likewise reflected, and among them the Englishman, who at that moment was intently observing myself. . . .

The crimson curtain being let down between the ladies and gentlemen, the cabin became a bedchamber for twenty persons, who were laid on shelves one above another. For a long time our various incommodities kept us all awake except five or six, who were accustomed to sleep nightly amid the uproar of their 491 own snoring, and had little to dread from any other species / of disturbance. It is a curious fact that these snorers had been the most quiet people in the boat while awake, and became peacebreakers only when others cease to be so, breathing tumult out of their repose. Would it were possible to affix a wind instrument to the nose, and thus make melody of a snore, so that a sleeping lover might serenade his mistress or a congregation snore a psalm tune! Other, though fainter, sounds than these contributed to my restlessness. My head was close to the crimson curtain, — the sexual division of the boat, — behind which I continually heard whispers and stealthy footsteps; the noise of a comb laid on the table or a slipper dropped on the floor; the twang, like a broken harpstring, caused by loosening a tight belt; the rustling of a gown in its descent; and the unlacing of a pair of stays. My ear seemed to have the properties of an eye; a visible image pestered my fancy in the darkness; the curtain was withdrawn between me and the western lady, who yet disrobed herself without a blush.

Finally all was hushed in that quarter. Still I was more broad awake than through the whole preceding day, and felt a feverish impulse to toss my limbs miles apart and appease the unquietness of mind by that of matter. Forgetting that my berth was hardly so wide as a coffin, I turned suddenly over, and fell like an avalanche on the floor, to the disturbance of the whole community of sleepers. As there were no bones broken, I blessed the accident and went on deck. A lantern was burning at each end of the boat, and one of the crew was stationed at the bows, keeping watch as mariners do on the ocean. Though the rain had ceased, the sky was all one cloud, and the darkness so intense that there seemed to be no world except 492 the / little space on which our lantern glimmered. Yet it was an impressive scene.

We were traversing the "long level," a dead flat between Utica and Syracuse, where the canal has not rise or fall enough to require a lock for nearly seventy miles. There can hardly be a more dismal tract of country. The forest which covers it consisting chiefly of white cedar, black ash, and other trees that live in excessive moisture, is now decayed and death-struck by the partial draining of the swamp into the great ditch of the canal. Sometimes, indeed, our lights were reflected from pools of stagnant water which stretched far in among the trunks of the trees, beneath dense masses of dark foliage. But generally the tall stems and intermingled branches were naked, and brought into strong relief amid the surrounding gloom by the whiteness of their decay. Often we beheld the prostrate form of some old sylvan giant which had fallen and crushed down smaller trees under its immense ruin. In spots where destruction had been riotous, the lanterns showed perhaps a hundred trunks, erect, half overthrown, extended along the ground, resting on their shattered limbs or tossing them desperately into the darkness, but all of one ashy white, all naked together, in desolate confusion. Thus growing out of the night as we drew nigh, and vanishing as we glided on, based on obscurity, and overhung and bounded by it, the scene was ghostlike—the very land of unsubstantial things, whither dreams might betake themselves when they quit the slumberer's brain.

My fancy found another emblem. The wild nature of America had been driven to this desert-place by the encroachments of civilized man. And even here, where 493 the savage queen was throned on the ruins of / her empire, did we penetrate, a vulgar and worldly throng, intruding on her latest solitude. In other lands decay sits among fallen palaces; but here her home is in the forests.

Looking ahead, I discerned a distant light, announcing the approach of another boat, which soon passed us, and proved to be a rusty old scow—just such a craft as the "Flying Dutchman" would navigate on the canal. Perhaps it was that celebrated personage himself whom I imperfectly distinguished at the helm, in a glazed cap and rough greatcoat, with a pipe in his mouth, leaving the fumes of tobacco a hundred yards behind. Shortly after our boatman blew a horn, sending a long and melancholy note through the forest avenue, as a signal for some watcher in the wilderness to be ready with a change of horses. We had proceeded a mile or two with our fresh team when the tow rope got entangled in a fallen branch on the edge of the canal and caused a momentary delay, during which I went to examine the phosphoric light of an old tree a little within the forest. It was not the first delusive radiance that I had followed.

The tree lay along the ground, and was wholly converted into a mass of diseased splendor, which threw a ghastliness around. Being full of conceits that night, I called it a frigid fire, a funeral light, illumining decay and death, an emblem of fame that gleams around the dead man without warming him, or of genius when it owes its brilliancy to moral rottenness, and was thinking that such ghostlike torches were just fit to light up this dead forest or to blaze coldly in tombs, when, starting from my abstraction, I looked up the canal. I recollected myself, and discovered the lanterns glimmering far away.

494   "Boat ahoy!" shouted I, making a trumpet of my closed fists.

Though the cry must have rung for miles along that hollow passage of the woods, it produced no effect. These packet boats make up for their snail-like pace by never loitering day nor night, especially for those who have paid their fare. Indeed, the captain had an interest in getting rid of me, for I was his creditor for a breakfast.

"They are gone, Heaven be praised!" ejaculated I; "for I cannot possibly overtake them. Here am I, on the 'long level,' at midnight, with the comfortable prospect of a walk to Syracuse, where my baggage will be left. And now to find a house or shed wherein to pass the night." So thinking aloud, I took a flambeau from the old tree, burning, but consuming not, to light my steps withal, and, like a jack-o'-the-lantern, set out on my midnight tour.

From Charles Dickens, *American Notes for General Circulation, Works of Charles Dickens.* The Riverside Edition, 29 vols. New York: Hurd and Houghton, 1874.

CHAPTER IX. . . . THE CANAL BOAT.

171   It still continued to rain heavily, and when we went down to the Canal-Boat (for that was the mode of conveyance by which we were to proceed) after dinner, the weather was as unpromising and obstinately wet as one would desire to see.

Nor was the sight of this canal-boat, in which we were to spend three or four days, by any means a cheerful one; as it involved some uneasy speculations concerning 172 the disposal of the passengers / at night, and opened a wide field of inquiry touching the other domestic arrangements of the establishment, which was sufficiently disconcerting.

However, there it was,—a barge with a little house in it, viewed from the outside; and a caravan at a fair, viewed from within: the gentlemen being accommodated, as the spectators usually are, in one of those locomotive museums of penny wonders; and the ladies being partitioned off by a red curtain, after the manner of the dwarfs and giants in the same establishments, whose private lives are passed in rather close exclusiveness.

We sat here, looking silently at the row of little tables, which extended down both sides of the cabin, and listening to the rain as it dripped and pattered on the boat, and plashed with a dismal merriment in the water, until the arrival of the railway-train, for whose final contribution to our stock of passengers, our departure was alone deferred. It brought a great many boxes, which were bumped and tossed upon the roof, almost as painfully as if they had been deposited on one's own head, without the intervention of a porter's knot; and several damp gentlemen, whose clothes, on their drawing round the stove, began to steam again. No doubt it would have been a thought more comfortable if the driving rain, which now poured down more soakingly than ever, had admitted of a window being opened, or if our number had been something less than thirty; but there was scarcely time to think as much, when a train of three horses was attached to the tow-rope, the boy upon the leader smacked his whip, the rudder creaked and groaned complainingly, and we had begun our journey.

CHAPTER X. SOME FURTHER ACCOUNT OF THE CANAL-BOAT, ITS DOMESTIC ECONOMY, AND ITS PASSENGERS. JOURNEY TO PITTSBURG ACROSS THE ALLEGHANY MOUNTAINS. PITTSBURG.

173   As it continued to rain most perseveringly, we all remained below: the damp gentlemen round the stove, gradually becoming mildewed by the action of the fire; and the dry gentlemen lying at full length upon the seats, or slumbering uneasily with their faces on the tables, or walking up and down the cabin, which it was barely possible for a man of the middle height to do, without making bald places on his head by scraping it against the roof. At about six o-clock, all the small tables were put together to form one long table, and everybody sat down to tea, coffee, bread, butter, salmon, shad, liver, steak, potatoes, pickles, ham, chops, black puddings, and sausages.

"Will you try," said my opposite neighbor, handing me a dish of potatoes, broken up in milk and butter,—"will you try some of these fixings?"

There are few words which perform such various duties as this word "fix." It is the Caleb Quotem of the American vocabulary. You call upon a gentleman in a country-town, and his help informs you that he is "fixing himself" just now, but will be down directly: by which you are to understand that he is dressing. 174 You inquire / on board a steamboat, of a fellow-passenger, whether breakfast will be ready soon, and he tells you he should think so, for when he was last below, they were "fixing the tables"; in other words, laying the cloth. You beg a porter to collect your luggage, and he entreats you not to be uneasy, for he'll "fix it presently"; and if you complain of indisposition, you are advised to have recourse to Doctor so and so, who will "fix you" in no time.

One night, I ordered a bottle of mulled wine at an hotel where I was staying, and waited a long time for it; at length it was put upon the table with an apology from the landlord that he feared it wasn't "fixed properly." And I recollect once, at a stage-coach dinner, overhearing a very stern gentleman demand of a waiter who presented him with a plate of underdone roast-beef, "whether he called *that* fixing God A'mighty's vittles?"

There is no doubt that the meal, at which the invitation was tendered to me which has occasioned this digression, was disposed of somewhat ravenously; and that the gentlemen thrust the broad-bladed knives and the two-pronged forks further down their throats than I ever saw the same weapons go before, except in the hands of a skilful juggler; but no man sat down until the ladies were seated; or omitted any little act of politeness which could contribute to their comfort. Nor did I ever once, on any occasion, anywhere, during my rambles in America, see a woman exposed to the slightest act of rudeness, incivility, or even inattention.

By the time the meal was over, the rain, which seemed to have worn itself out by coming down so fast, was nearly over too; and it became feasible to go on deck, which was a great relief, notwithstanding its being a very small deck, and 175 being rendered still smaller by the / luggage, which was heaped together in the middle under a tarpaulin covering; leaving, on either side, a path so narrow, that it became a science to walk to and fro without tumbling overboard into the canal. It was somewhat embarrassing at first, too, to have to duck nimbly every five minutes whenever the man at the helm cried "Bridge!" and sometimes, when the cry was "Low Bridge," to lie down nearly flat. But custom familiarizes one to anything, and there were so many bridges that it took a very short time to get used to this.

As night came on, and we drew in sight of the first range of hills, which are the outposts of the Alleghany Mountains, the scenery, which had been uninteresting hitherto, became more bold and striking. The wet ground reeked and smoked, after the heavy fall of rain; and the croaking of the frogs (whose noise in these parts is almost incredible) sounded as though a million of fairy teams with bells, were travelling through the air, and keeping pace with us. The night was cloudy yet, but moonlight too; and when we crossed the Susquehanna River — over which there is an extraordinary wooden bridge with two galleries, one above the other, so that even there, two boat-teams meeting, may pass without confusion — it was wild and grand.

I have mentioned my having been in some uncertainty and doubt, at first, relative to the sleeping arrangements on board this boat. I remained in the same vague state of mind until ten o'clock or thereabouts, when going below, I found suspended on either side of the cabin, three long tiers of hanging book-shelves, designed apparently for volumes of the small octavo size. Looking with greater attention at these contrivances (wondering to find such literary preparations in such a 176 place), I descried / on each shelf a sort of microscopic sheet and blanket; then I began dimly to comprehend that the passengers were the library, and that they were to be arranged, edgewise, on these shelves, till morning.

I was assisted to this conclusion by seeing some of them gathered round the master of the boat, at one of the tables, drawing lots with all the anxieties and passions of gamesters depicted in their countenances; while others, with small pieces of cardboard in their hands, were groping among the shelves in search of numbers corresponding with those they had drawn. As soon as any gentleman found his number, he took possession of it by immediately undressing himself and crawling into bed. The rapidity with which an agitated gambler subsided into a snoring slumberer, was one of the most singular effects I have ever witnessed. As to the ladies, they were already abed, behind the red curtain, which was carefully drawn and pinned up the centre; though as every cough, or sneeze, or whisper, behind this curtain, was perfectly audible before it, we had still a lively consciousness of their society.

The politeness of the person in authority had secured to me a shelf in a nook near this red curtain, in some degree removed from the great body of sleepers: to which place I retired, with many acknowledgments to him for his attention. I found it, on after-measurement, just the width of an ordinary sheet of Bath post letter-paper; and I was at first in some uncertainty as to the best means of getting into it. But the shelf being a bottom one, I finally determined on lying upon the floor, rolling gently in, stopping immediately I touched the mattress, and remaining for the night with that side uppermost, whatever it might be. Luckily, I came 177 upon my back / at exactly the right moment. I was much alarmed on looking upward, to see, by the shape of his half yard of sacking (which his weight had bent into an exceedingly tight bag), that there was a very heavy gentleman above me, whom the slender cords seemed quite incapable of holding; and I could not help reflecting upon the grief of my wife and family in the event of his coming down in the night. But as I could not have got up again without a severe bodily struggle, which might have alarmed the ladies; and as I had nowhere to go to even if I had; I shut my eyes upon the danger, and remained there.

One of two remarkable circumstances is indisputably a fact, with reference to that class of society who travel in these boats. Either they carry their restlessness to such a pitch that they never sleep at all; or they expectorate in dreams, which would be a remarkable mingling of the real and ideal. All night long, and every night, on this canal, there was a perfect storm and tempest of spitting; and once my coat, being in the very centre of a hurricane sustained by five gentlemen, (which moved vertically, strictly carrying out Reid's Theory of the Law of Storms,) I was fain the next morning to lay it on the deck, and rub it down with fair water before it was in a condition to be worn again.

Between five and six o'clock in the morning we got up, and some of us went on deck, to give them an opportunity of taking the shelves down; while others, the morning being very cold, crowded round the rusty stove, cherishing the newly kindled fire, and filling the grate with those voluntary contributions of which they had been so liberal all night. The washing accommodations were primitive. There 178 was a tin ladle chained to the deck / with which every gentleman who thought it necessary to cleanse himself (many were superior to this weakness) fished the dirty water out of the canal, and poured it into a tin basin, secured in like manner. There was also a jack-towel. And, hanging up before a little looking-glass in the bar, in the immediate vicinity of the bread and cheese and biscuits, were a public comb and hairbrush.

At eight o-clock, the shelves being taken down and put away, and the tables joined together, everybody sat down to the tea, coffee, bread, butter, salmon, shad, liver, steak, potatoes, pickles, ham, chops, black puddings, and sausages, all over again. Some were fond of compounding this variety, and having it all on their plates at once. As each gentleman got through his own personal amount of tea, coffee, bread, butter, salmon, shad, liver, steak, potatoes, pickles, ham, chops, black puddings, and sausages, he rose up and walked off. When everybody had done with everything, the fragments were cleared away; and one of the waiters appearing anew in the character of a barber, shaved such of the company as desired to be shaved; while the remainder looked on, or yawned over their newspapers. Dinner was breakfast again, without the tea and coffee; and supper and breakfast were identical.

There was a man on board this boat, with a light fresh-colored face, and a pepper-and-salt suit of clothes, who was the most inquisitive fellow that can possibly be imagined. He never spoke otherwise than interrogatively. He was an embodied inquiry. Sitting down or standing up, still or moving, walking the deck or taking his meals, there he was, with a great note of interrogation in each eye, 179 two in his cocked ears, two more in his / turned-up nose and chin, at least half a dozen more about the corners of his mouth, and the largest one of all in his hair, which was brushed pertly off his forehead in a flaxen clump. Every button in his clothes said, "Eh? What's that? Did you speak? Say that again, will you?" He was always wide awake, like the enchanted bride who drove her husband frantic; always restless; always thirsting for answers; perpetually seeking and never finding. There never was such a curious man.

I wore a fur great-coat at that time, and before we were well clear of the wharf, he questioned me concerning it, and its price, and where I bought it, and when, and what fur it was, and what it weighed, and what it cost. Then he took notice of my watch, and asked what *that* cost, and whether it was a French watch, and where I got it, and how I got it, and whether I bought it or had it given me, and how it went, and where the keyhole was, and when I wound it, every night or every morning, and whether I ever forgot to wind it at all, and if I did, what then? Where had I been to last, and where was I going next, and where was I going after that, and had I seen the President, and what did he say, and what did I say, and what did he say when I had said that? Eh? Lor now! do tell!

Finding that nothing would satisfy him, I evaded his questions after the first score or two, and in particular pleaded ignorance respecting the name of the fur whereof the coat was made. I am unable to say whether this was the reason, but that coat fascinated him ever afterwards; he usually kept close behind me as I walked, and moved as I moved, that he might look at it the better; and he frequently dived into narrow places after me at the risk of his life, that he might have 180 the satis- / faction of passing his hand up the back, and rubbing it the wrong way.

We had another odd specimen on board, of a different kind. This was a thin-faced, spare-figured man of middle age and stature, dressed in a dusty drabbish-colored suit, such as I never saw before. He was perfectly quiet during the first part of the journey: indeed I don't remember having so much as seen him until he was brought out by circumstances, as great men often are. The conjunction of events which made him famous, happened, briefly, thus.

The canal extends to the foot of the mountain, and there, of course, it stops; the passengers being conveyed across it by land-carriage, and taken on afterwards by another canal-boat, the counterpart of the first, which awaits them on the other side. There are two canal lines of passage-boats; one is called The Express, and one (a cheaper one) The Pioneer. The Pioneer gets first to the mountain, and waits for the Express people to come up; both sets of passengers being conveyed across

it at the same time. We were the Express company; but when we had crossed the mountain, and had come to the second boat, the proprietors took it into their heads to draft all the Pioneers into it likewise, so that we were five-and-forty at least, and the accession of passengers was not at all of that kind which improved the prospect of sleeping at night. Our people grumbled at this, as people do in such cases; but suffered the boat to be towed off with the whole freight aboard nevertheless; and away we went down the canal. At home, I should have protested lustily, but being a foreigner here, I held my peace. Not so this passenger. He
181 cleft a path among the people on deck (we were nearly all on deck), / and without addressing anybody whomsoever, soliloquized as follows:—

"This may suit *you*, this may, but it don't suit *me*. This may be all very well with Down Easters, and men of Boston raising, but it won't suit my figure no how, and no two ways about *that;* and so I tell you. Now, I'm from the brown forests of the Mississippi, *I* am, and when the sun shines on me, it does shine—a little. It don't glimmer where *I* live, the sun don't. No. I'm a brown forester, I am. I a'n't a Johnny Cake. There are no smooth skins where I live. We're rough men there. Rather. If Down Easters and men of Boston raising like this, I'm glad of it, but I'm none of that raising nor of that breed. No. This company wants a little fixing, *it* does. I'm the wrong sort of man for 'em, *I* am. They won't like me, *they* won't. This is piling of it up, a little too mountainous, this is." At the end of every one of these short sentences he turned upon his heel, and walked the other way; checking himself abruptly when he had finished another short sentence, and turning back again.

It is impossible for me to say what terrific meaning was hidden in the words of this brown forester, but I know that the other passengers looked on in a sort of admiring horror, and that presently the boat was put back to the wharf, and as many of the Pioneers as could be coaxed or bullied into going away, were got rid of.

When we started again, some of the boldest spirits on board made bold to say to the obvious occasion of this improvement in our prospects, "Much obliged to you, sir:" whereunto the brown forester (waving his hand, and still walking up and down as before) replied, "No you a'n't. You're none o' my raising. You may
182 act for / yourselves, *you* may. I have pinted out the way. Down Easters and Johnny Cakes can follow if they please. I a'n't a Johnny Cake, *I* a'n't. I am from the brown forests of the Mississippi, *I* am"—and so on, as before. He was unanimously voted one of the tables for his bed at night—there is a great contest for the tables—in consideration of his public services; and he had the warmest corner by the stove throughout the rest of the journey. But I never could find out that he did anything except sit there; nor did I hear him speak again until, in the midst of the bustle and turmoil of getting the luggage ashore in the dark at Pittsburg, I stumbled over him as he sat smoking a cigar on the cabin-steps, and heard him muttering to himself, with a short laugh of defiance, "I a'n't a Johnny Cake, *I* a'n't. I'm from the brown forests of the Mississippi, *I* am, damme!" I am inclined to argue from this, that he had never left off saying so; but I could not make affidavit of that part of the story, if required to do so by my Queen and Country.

As we have not reached Pittsburg yet, however, in the order of our narrative, I may go on to remark that breakfast was perhaps the least desirable meal of the day; as an addition to the many savory odors arising from the eatables already mentioned, there were whiffs of gin, whiskey, brandy, and rum, from the little bar

hard by, and a decided seasoning of stale tobacco. Many of the gentlemen passengers were far from particular in respect of their linen, which was in some cases
as yellow as the little rivulets that had trickled from the corners of their mouths
in chewing, and dried there. Nor was the atmosphere quite free from zephyr whis-
183 perings of the thirty beds which had just been cleared away, / and of which we
were further and more pressingly reminded by the occasional appearance on the
table-cloth of a kind of Game, not mentioned in the Bill of Fare.

And yet despite these oddities — and even they had, for me at least, a humor
of their own — there was much in this mode of travelling which I heartily enjoyed
at the time, and look back upon with great pleasure. Even the running up, bare-
necked, at five o'clock in the morning, from the tainted cabin to the dirty deck;
scooping up the icy water, plunging one's head into it, and drawing it out, all
fresh and glowing with the cold; was a good thing. The fast, brisk walk upon the
towing-path between that time and breakfast, when every vein and artery seemed
to tingle with health; the exquisite beauty of the opening day, when light came
gleaming off from everything; the lazy motion of the boat, when one lay idly on
the deck, looking through, rather than at, the deep blue sky; the gliding on at night,
so noiselessly, past frowning hills, sullen with dark trees, and sometimes angry in
one red burning spot high up, where unseen men lay crouching round a fire; the
shining out of the bright stars, undisturbed by noise of wheels or steam, or any
other sound than the liquid rippling of the water as the boat went on: all these
were pure delights.

Then, there were new settlements and detached log-cabins and frame-houses,
full of interest for strangers from an old country: cabins with simple ovens, outside, made of clay; and lodgings for the pigs nearly as good as many of the human
quarters; broken windows, patched with worn-out hats, old clothes, old boards,
fragments of blankets and paper; and home-made dressers standing in the open
air without the door, whereon was ranged the household store, not hard to count,
184 of earthen jars and pots. / The eye was pained to see the stumps of great trees
thickly strewn in every field of wheat, and seldom to lose the eternal swamp and
dull morass, with hundreds of rotten trunks and twisted branches steeped in its
unwholesome water. It was quite sad and oppressive to come upon great tracts
where settlers had been burning down the trees, and where their wounded bodies
lay about like those of murdered creatures, while here and there some charred
and blackened giant reared aloft two withered arms, and seemed to call down
curses on his foes. Sometimes, at night, the way wound through some lonely gorge,
like a mountain-pass in Scotland, shining and coldly glittering in the light of the
moon, and so closed in by high steep hills all round, that there seemed to be no
egress save through the narrower path by which we had come, until one rugged
hill-side seemed to open, and, shutting out the moonlight as we passed into its
gloomy throat, wrapped our new course in shade and darkness.

We had left Harrisburg on Friday. On Sunday morning we arrived at the foot
of the mountain, which is crossed by railroad. There are ten inclined planes; five
ascending, and five descending; the carriages are dragged up the former, and let
slowly down the latter, by means of stationary engines; the comparatively level
spaces between being traversed, sometimes by horse, and sometimes by engine
power, as the case demands. Occasionally the rails are laid upon the extreme verge
of a giddy precipice; and looking from the carriage-window, the traveller gazes
sheer down, without a stone or scrap of fence between, into the mountain depths

below. The journey is very carefully made, however; only two carriages travelling together; and, while proper precautions are taken, is not to be dreaded for its dangers.

185   It was very pretty travelling thus, at a rapid pace along the heights of the mountain in a keen wind, to look down into a valley full of light and softness: catching glimpses, through the tree-tops, of scattered cabins; children running to the doors; dogs bursting out to bark, whom we could see without hearing; terrified pigs scampering homewards; families sitting out in their rude gardens; cows gazing upward with a stupid indifference; men in their shirt-sleeves looking on at their unfinished houses, planning out to-morrow's work; and we riding onward, high above them, like a whirlwind. It was amusing, too, when we had dined, and rattled down a steep pass, having no other moving power than the weight of the carriages themselves, to see the engine released, long after us, come buzzing down alone, like a great insect, its back of green and gold so shining in the sun, that if it had spread a pair of wings and soared away, no one would have had occasion, as I fancied, for the least surprise. But it stopped short of us in a very business-like manner when we reached the canal; and before we left the wharf, went panting up this hill again, with the passengers who had waited our arrival for the means of traversing the road by which we had come.

   On the Monday evening, furnace-fires and clanking hammers on the banks of the canal, warned us that we approached the termination of this part of our journey. After going through another dreamy place — a long aqueduct across the Alleghany River, which was stranger than the bridge at Harrisburg, being a vast low wooden chamber full of water — we emerged upon that ugly confusion of backs of buildings and crazy galleries and stairs, which always abuts on water, whether it be river, sea, canal, or ditch: and were at Pittsburg.

From William Dean Howells, *A Boy's Town.* New York: Harper & Brothers, 1890.

40   Beyond the pork-houses, and up farther towards the canal, there were some houses under the Basin banks. They were good places for the fever-and-ague which people had in those days without knowing it was malaria, or suffering it to interfere much with the pleasure and business of life; but they seemed to my boy bowers of delight, especially one where there was a bear, chained to a weeping-willow, and another where there was a fishpond with gold-fish in it. He expected this bear to get loose and eat him, but that could not spoil his pleasure in seeing the bear stand on his hind-legs and open his red mouth, as I have seen bears do when you wound them up by a keyhole in the side. In fact, a toy bear is very much like a real bear, and safer to have round. The boys were always wanting to go and look at this bear, but he was not so exciting as the daily arrival of the Dayton packet. To my boy's young vision this craft was of such incomparable lightness and grace as no yacht of Mr. Burgess's could rival. When she came in of a summer evening her deck was thronged with people, and the captain stood with his right foot on the spring-catch that held the tow-rope. The water curled away on either side of her sharp prow, that cut its way onward at the full rate of five miles an hour, and the team came swinging down the tow-path at a gallant

41 trot, the driver sitting the hindmost horse of three, and / cracking his long-lashed whip with loud explosions, as he whirled its snaky spirals in the air. All the boys

in town were there, meekly proud to be ordered out of his way, to break and fly before his volleyed oaths and far before his horses' feet; and suddenly the captain pressed his foot on the spring and released the tow-rope. The driver kept on to the stable with unslackened speed, and the line followed him, swishing and skating over the water, while the steersman put his helm hard aport, and the packet rounded to, and swam softly and slowly up to her moorings. No steamer arrives from Europe now with such thrilling majesty.

The canal-boatmen were all an heroic race, and the boys humbly hoped that some day, if they proved worthy, they might grow up to be drivers; not indeed packet-drivers; they were not so conceited as that; but freight-boat drivers, of two horses, perhaps, but gladly of one. High or low, the drivers had a great deal of leisure, which commended their calling to the boyish fancy; and my boy saw them, with a longing to speak to them, even to approach them, never satisfied, while they amused the long summer afternoon in the shade of the tavern by a game of skill peculiar to them. They put a tack into a whiplash, and then, whirling it round and round, drove it to the head in a target marked out on the weather-boarding. Some of them had a perfect aim; and in fact it was a very pretty feat, and well worth seeing.

. . . .

239 He now looked forward eagerly to helping on the new paper, and somewhat proudly to living in the larger place the family were going to. The moment it was decided he began to tell the boys that he was going to live in a city, and he felt that it gave him distinction. He had nothing but joy in it, and he did not dream that as the time drew near it could be sorrow. But when it came at last, and he was to leave the house, the town, the boys, he found himself deathly homesick. The parting days were days of gloom; the parting was an anguish of bitter tears. Nothing consoled him but the fact that they were going all the way to the new place in a canal-boat, which his father chartered for the trip. My boy and his brother had once gone to Cincinnati in a canal-boat, with a friendly captain of their acquaintance, and, though they were both put to sleep in a berth so narrow that when they turned they fell out on the floor, the glory of the adventure remained with him, and he could have thought of nothing more delightful than such another voyage. The household goods were piled up in the middle of the boat, and the family had a cabin forward, which seemed immense to the children. They played in it and ran races up and down the long canal-boat roof, where their father and mother sometimes put their chairs and sat to admire the scenery.

240 As my boy could remember very few incidents of this voyage afterwards, I dare say he spent a great part of it with his face in a book, and was aware of the landscape only from time to time when he lifted his eyes from the story he was reading. That was apt to be the way with him; and before he left the Boy's Town the world within claimed him more and more. He ceased to be that eager comrade he had once been; sometimes he left his book with a sigh; and he saw much of the outer world through a veil of fancies quivering like an autumn haze between him and its realities, softening their harsh outlines, and giving them a fairy coloring. I think he would sometimes have been better employed in looking directly at them; but he had to live his own life, and I cannot live it over for him. The season was the one of all others best fitted to win him to the earth, and in a measure it did. It was spring, and along the towpath strutted the large, glossy blackbirds which had just come back, and made the boys sick with longing to kill them, they

offered such good shots. But the boys had no powder with them, and at any rate
the captain would not have stopped his boat, which was rushing on at the rate
of two miles an hour, to let them pick up a bird, if they had hit it. They were sufficiently provisioned without the game, however; the mother had baked bread,
and boiled a ham, and provided sugar-cakes in recognition of the holiday character
of the voyage, and they had the use of the boat cooking-stove for their tea and
coffee. The boys had to content themselves with such sense of adventure as they
could get out of going ashore when the boat was passing through the locks, or
241 staying aboard and seeing the water burst and plunge in around the / boat. They
had often watched this thrilling sight at the First Lock, but it had a novel interest
now. As their boat approached the lock, the lower gates were pushed open by men
who set their breasts to the long sweeps or handles of the gates, and when the
boat was fairly inside of the stone-walled lock they were closed behind her. Then
the upper gates, which opened against the dull current, and were kept shut by
its pressure, were opened a little, and the waters rushed and roared into the lock,
and began to lift the boat. The gates were opened wider and wider, till the waters
poured a heavy cataract into the lock, where the boat tossed on their increasing
volume, and at last calmed themselves to the level within. Then the boat passed
out through the upper gates, on even water, and the voyage to the next lock began.
At first it was rather awful, and the little children were always afraid when they
came to a lock, but the boys enjoyed it after the first time. They would have liked
to take turns driving the pair of horses that drew the boat, but it seemed too bold
a wish, and I think they never proposed it; they did not ask, either, to relieve the
man at the helm.

They arrived safely at their journey's end, without any sort of accident. They
had made the whole forty miles in less than two days, and were all as well as when
they started, without having suffered for a moment from seasickness. The boat
drew up at the tow-path just before the stable belonging to the house which the
father had already taken, and the whole family at once began helping the crew
put the things ashore.

The Paper

The problems the student encountered in the writing of his paper can best
be considered after you have read the following complete paper.

Packet Boat Travel on American Canals

Passengers on the packet boats on nineteenth-century American
canals must have had—but for some bumping in the locks—the smooth-
est ride in the history of American public transportation. Perhaps they also had the slowest. The legal speed of a canal boat on
the Erie was four miles an hour, for at any greater speed the earthen
banks of the canal were endangered by the wash of the boat.[1] Packet
boats, however, ran day and night and Sundays, often with relays

[1]Alvin F. Harlow, Old Towpaths (New York, 1926), p. 364.

of fresh horses every twelve or fifteen miles. They had precedence at the locks, and they were allowed to pass slower boats.[2] They partly made up in persistence what they lacked in speed; a packet boat might cover eighty miles in twenty-four hours, including delays at towns and locks.[3]

Packet boats were not the only means of canal travel. Many persons traveled on the line boats, designed to carry both freight and passengers. The line boats were slower and less expensive than the packet boats, but apparently they had somewhat roomier and more comfortable quarters. A family moving to another town might charter a line boat to carry both themselves and their furniture; William Dean Howells tells of such a journey on an Ohio canal in his A Boy's Town.[4] But the packet boats carried a large share of the passenger traffic, and they were profitable and highly competitive. In the 1820s passenger fares on the Erie were four cents a mile, including meals.[5]

The largest packet boats were 80 by 14 feet (barely clearing the locks of 90 by 15 feet), with almost all the deck space taken up with the many-windowed cabin, and only very small lower decks at bow and stern. The top of the cabin was flat and made a sort of upper deck upon which the passengers sat or walked about in good weather. The boats were pulled ordinarily by two or three horses in tandem, with the "hoggee" or driver riding the last. There was a bow man or lookout in front, a helmsman at the stern. A steward, a cook, and a cabin boy looked after the needs of the passengers. The cook, usually a Negro, might double as barkeeper. Over all was the captain, a personage of dignity and self-importance.[6]

Travelers' accounts of journeys on canal packets vary a good deal, but characteristically they weigh some enjoyment against rather more unpleasantness. Harriet Martineau records in her Retrospect of Western Travel a journey on the Erie in the 1830s. Although she says her packet was no place for a lady, she found her trip not entirely unpleasant:

> On fine days it is pleasant enough sitting outside (except for having to duck under the bridges every quarter of an hour, under penalty of having one's head crushed to atoms), and in dark evenings the approach of the boatlights on the water is a pretty sight; but the horrors of night and of wet days more

[2]Samuel Hopkins Adams, The Erie Canal (New York, 1953), p. 146.
[3]Ronald E. Shaw, Erie Water West (Lexington, Ky., 1966), p. 214.
[4]A Boy's Town (New York, 1890), pp. 238–241.
[5]Shaw, p. 214.
[6]See Adams, p. 145.

than compensate for all the advantages these vehicles can
boast. The heat and the noise, the known vicinity of a compressed crowd, lying packed like herrings in a barrel, the
bumping against the sides of the locks, and the hissing of
water therein like an inundation, startling one from sleep;
these things are very disagreeable.[7]

Miss Martineau adds that she "suffered under an additional annoyance in the presence of sixteen Presbyterian clergymen," but that
was probably an unusual difficulty.

For Miss Martineau the locks were apparently more an irritation
than an interest; for Howells as a boy of twelve passing through a
lock was an exciting experience. When a boat approached a lock,
he tells us, "the lower gates were pushed open by men who set their
breasts to the long sweeps or handles of the gates." When the boat
was inside the lock, those gates were closed, and the upper gates
were opened gradually against the current, until "the waters
poured a heavy cataract into the lock, where the boat tossed on
their increasing volume, and at last calmed themselves to the level
within" so that the boat could pass through the upper gates and
proceed on its way. Howells tells us that "at first it was rather
awful," but thereafter a pleasure to his brother and to himself.[8]
Howells is remembering a time of life, however, in which many experiences are new and delightful.

Among the accounts of canal boat travel by more mature travelers,
there are two by famous writers—Nathaniel Hawthorne and Charles
Dickens—which may be the most vivid records of canal journeys that
have come down to us. The accounts are alike in some respects. Both
writers are making copy of their experiences, both seem mannered
and self-conscious, but both have the professional writer's eye
for significant detail.

Hawthorne's "The Canal Boat" was first printed in The New England Magazine in 1835. It seems to be an account of a trip made a
year or two earlier; then Hawthorne was about thirty, still un-
married, and not well known as a writer. He describes his embarka-
tion on the Erie in this fashion:

Behold us, then, fairly afloat, with three horses harnessed
to our vessel. . . . Bound to a distant port, we had neither
chart nor compass, nor cared about the wind, nor felt the
heaving of a billow . . . in our adventurous navigation of an
interminable mud puddle. . . . Yet there is variety enough,
both on the surface of the canal and along its banks, to amuse

[7]Quoted in Shaw, p. 209.
[8]Howells, p. 241.

the traveller, if an overpowering tedium did not deaden his
perceptions.9

Tedium did not overpower Hawthorne's perceptions, and he records
a good deal of the variety of the life on the canal and canalside.

Hawthorne observed, for instance, the many line boats with a
cabin at each end, and freight piled between; occasionally "a black
and rusty-looking vessel" that was at once freight boat and house-
boat, so that the family carried "their own fireside with them";
and once a rude craft manned by three silent Indians (pp. 485–486).
He flirted with a pretty Swiss girl on a line boat overtaken by his
packet, one of a little colony of Swiss migrating to Michigan; and
the two laughed "heartily at each other's unintelligible wit"
(p. 486). Swiss immigrants traveled the Erie from the beginning of
its operation;10 any packet might have overtaken a boatload of
them.

Life along the Erie, Hawthorne realized, offered high con-
trasts. He considered the lonely cottages canalside, where one
might see a "lean and aguish" woman "like poverty personified";
again a thriving little community grown up around a lock; or again
Utica, one of the bustling new cities the canal had made, with its
"eager and hurrying spirit" (p. 487). Yet another time, in the evening, he fancied that "a rusty old scow [was] just such a craft as the
'Flying Dutchman' would navigate on the canal," and that perhaps
the helmsman was he (p. 493).

Hawthorne's account of the life aboard the boat and the accommo-
dation for passengers is typical enough. Like other travelers,
he had to throw himself nearly flat as the boat approached one of
the frequent "occupation bridges" over the canal;11 and he found
the tedium of the journey relieved by the minor catastrophe that
overtook a Virginia schoolmaster who, intent on his Virgil, forgot
to duck (p. 488). He enjoyed his meals (p. 489)–the food on packet
boats seems generally to have been good.12 The cabin on his packet
boat, by day sitting and dining room, was at night divided by a crimson curtain, with the men on the one side of it and the women on the

---

9Mosses from an Old Manse, p. 485, in Works, Riverside Edition, Boston: Houghton, Mifflin and Company, 1883. Subsequent
page references to "The Canal Boat" will appear parenthetically
in the text.

10Harlow, p. 117.

11Along the Erie every farmer whose land was divided by the
canal had a bridge built for him by the State of New York. See Adams,
pp. 71–72.

12See Shaw, pp. 207 and 211.

other. The passengers slept on shelf-like berths, "hardly so wide
as a coffin," one above another, probably in three tiers. Hawthorne
does not remark, as other travelers do, the fetid atmosphere of the
cabin, but then his packet boat carried only twenty passengers.
He does remark the annoyance of the five or six snorers about him.
And he was disturbed by his proximity to the crimson curtain—"the
sexual division of the boat"—and could not banish from his consciousness the vague rustlings from its other side: "my ear," he
says, "seemed to have the properties of an eye; a visible image pestered my fancy in the darkness" (p. 491). During the night he fell
out of his berth—Howells, too, remarks such an accident.[13]

Among the passengers was a note-taking Englishman, who, Hawthorne fancied, would write a book of American travels: "He would
hold up an imaginary mirror, wherein our reflected faces would
appear ugly and ridiculous, yet still retain an undeniable likeness to the originals" (p. 489). By 1835 other British travelers
had written accounts of American journeys, but in his account of
the English traveler Hawthorne seems almost to prophesy Charles
Dickens' American Notes for General Circulation (1842), which,
although never malicious, has the quality of brilliant exaggera-
tion and caricature we know in his novels. American Notes includes
the record of Dickens' journey on the Pennsylvania Main Line Canal
from Harrisburg westward to Pittsburg in 1842.[14]

On a rainy afternoon Dickens embarked on his packet boat, "a
barge with a little house on it," with baggage piled on its flat
roof-deck, and found his rain-soaked fellow passengers steaming
in the cabin, the sexes separated by a red curtain. At six the small
tables were pushed together "and everybody sat down to tea, coffee,
bread, butter, salmon, shad, liver, steak, potatoes, pickles, ham,
chops, black puddings, and sausages," all on the table at once.
And this appalling collection of dishes was offered unchanged at
the other two meals. Dickens remarks both the barbarous way in
which his fellow male passengers took in their food, and their un-
failing courtesy to women (pp. 172-174). After supper, the weather
having cleared, some of the passengers went on deck, and Dickens
learned to duck at the cry of "Bridge!" and to throw himself nearly
flat at "Low Bridge!" (pp. 174-175)

In the moonlight of this evening Dickens' boat crossed the Susquehanna River, over which there was a bridge 2,231 feet long that

---

[13]Howells, 239. And see Shaw, p. 208.
[14]American Notes for General Circulation, pp. 171-185, in
Works, Riverside Edition, New York: Hurd and Houghton, 1874. Subsequent page references to American Notes will appear parenthetically in the text.

carried a sort of two-story towpath.[15] On this bridge the canal
boat horses walked and pulled the boat across the river. Dickens
describes it as an "extraordinary wooden bridge with two galleries, one above the other, so that even there, two boat-teams meeting, may pass without confusion" and says that the experience was
"wild and grand" (p. 175).

Returning to the cabin at bed time, Dickens found three tiers of
berths let down and ready for occupancy, berths so narrow that he
pretends to have thought them bookshelves. The passengers were
drawing lots for them, but Dickens, apparently as a distinguished
visitor, was accorded a lower "in some degree removed from the great
body of sleepers," and near the red curtain. Every sound from behind it was audible—like Hawthorne he had a "lively consciousness"
of the proximity of his feminine neighbors. Since his berth was
virtually on the floor, he could hardly fall out of it, but he was
alarmed by "the very heavy gentleman above . . . whom the slender
cords seemed quite incapable of holding." He does not complain of
snorers, but he mentions them. He does complain, here as frequently
elsewhere in American Notes, of the "tempest of spitting," although one can hardly suppose that his fellow passengers chewed
tobacco in their sleep. He got up between five and six, and washed
on deck with water he drew himself from the canal (pp. 175–178).
Altogether, the accommodations were hardly luxurious; nineteenth-
century travelers encountered little luxury.

But if Dickens found the packet boat uncomfortable, he found
some things about his journey that he "heartily enjoyed." Even
the morning wash was invigorating, and after it he delighted in a
brisk morning walk along the towpath, keeping up with the boat and,
probably, regaining it by dropping to it from an occupation bridge.
(Passengers evidently often took such walks to relieve their tedium: Hawthorne in "The Canal Boat" purports to have been left behind while he was ashore and inattentive.) Dickens especially
enjoyed watching from the deck the countryside lazily pass by him,
changing its aspects through the day and into the night as his boat
moved silently through newly settled regions—although he was sometimes disturbed by the squalor in which the new settlers lived and
pained at the burning of forests to make farm land (pp. 183–185).
And he enjoyed, too, the Allegheny Portage which began at Hollidaysburg—an experience that he could have had only on the Main
Line Canal.

At Hollidaysburg the canal ended at the foot of a mountain ridge.
The passengers disembarked and were carried in railway carriages

15Harlow, p. 102.

operated by a stationary engine over the ridge up and down a series
of incline planes. On the comparatively level spaces between
slopes the carriages were hauled "sometimes by horse, and sometimes by engine power," Dickens says, as the case demanded. On the
Allegheny Portage at some period the canal boats themselves were
hauled in sections over the mountain: Alvin F. Harlow speaks of
"the remarkable jointed packet boats, which could be cut in halves
and carried over the 36-mile, mountain-climbing railroad on cars
and set afloat again."[16] But Dickens clearly does not describe
any such operation: "looking from the carriage-window," he says,
"the traveller gazes sheer down . . . into the mountain depths below" (p. 184).

At Johnstown, when the Allegheny Portage had been made, the
packet boat management attempted to put the passengers of Dickens'
boat and of another that had arrived at Hollidaysburg at nearly the
same time into one boat for the rest of the canal journey to Pittsburg. The passengers grumbled, and Dickens says that, had he been
at home, he would have "protested lustily." But the effective protest, the protest that persuaded the captain to put back to the
wharf and reduce the number of passengers, was made by a Westerner
—a fine specimen of a sort we know elsewhere in American literature
and folklore. Pacing back and forth the while, the Westerner spoke
in frontier brag:

> "This may suit you, this may, but it don't suit me. This may be
> all very well with Down Easters, and men of Boston raising, but
> it won't suit my figure no how, and no two ways about that; and
> so I tell you. Now, I'm from the brown forests of the Missis-
> sippi, I am, and when the sun shines on me, it does shine—a
> little. It don't glimmer where I live, the sun don't. No. I'm
> a brown forester, I am. I a'n't a Johnny Cake. There are no
> smooth skins where I live. We're rough men there. . . . This
> company wants a little fixing, it does. I'm the wrong sort of
> man for 'em." (p. 181)

The passage reminds one of the raftsmen's brag in Chapter iii of
Life on the Mississippi, and indeed Mark Twain is there represent-
ing persons of about the place and period of Dickens' fellow passenger.

After the contretemps at Johnstown, Dickens and his party proceeded without incident and arrived at last at the long aqueduct
across the Allegheny River. The aqueducts were striking features
of the American canals: they were essentially sections of the
canals mounted on bridges. The aqueduct across the Allegheny was,

---

[16]Harlow, p. 306. See also p. 363.

Dickens says, "another dreamy place . . . a vast wooden chamber full of water" (p. 185). Having crossed the aqueduct, Dickens disembarked at Pittsburg. He had left Harrisburg on a Friday afternoon and arrived in Pittsburg on Monday evening. The highway distance between the two cities today is 200 miles, an easy and short day's journey by car.[17]

But speed is after all a relative thing, and in the canal era packet boats had the romance of travel and of far places. Howells remembers the arrival of a packet boat in Hamilton, Ohio, when he was a boy in the late 1840s:

> When she came in of a summer evening her deck was thronged with people, and the captain stood with his right foot on the spring-catch that held the tow-rope. The water curled away on either side of her sharp prow, that cut its way onward at the full rate of five miles an hour, and the team came swinging down the tow-path at a gallant trot, the driver sitting the hindmost horse of three, and cracking his long-lashed whip with loud explosions. . . . All the boys in town were there, meekly proud to be ordered out of his way. . . . No steamer arrives from Europe now with such thrilling majesty.[18]

To the boys of Howells' time and place, "the canal-boatmen were all an heroic race"; and it was the boys' ambition to be canal-boatmen, men who had the romance of travel about them, as in another region it was the ambition of Mark Twain's boyhood companions to be steamboat men on the Mississippi.

In their ambition to be canal-boatmen the boys were recognizing an American achievement. Part of the romance came from the sense of the importance of the canals in developing this frontier continent. Americans were vastly proud of the network of canals from the Eastern seaboard to Illinois and as far south as Virginia— 3,326 miles of them by 1840.[19] The packet boats that plied on those canals were carrying persons busy about the development of the new country and the opening of the West. But those busy persons were not writers, and they left no record comparable to Hawthorne's account of an aimless vacation journey, or to Dickens' hasty notes on canal travel and travelers in Pennsylvania.

[17]Travel on the Main Line Canal must have been slower than on the Erie, for the Main Line Canal passed through difficult terrain, and had in its entire length 174 locks as against the Erie's eighty-four (George Rogers Taylor, The Transportation Revolution 1815-1860, New York, 1951, p. 44). Curiously Dickens does not mention any lock. Most of Hawthorne's journey was on the level stretch of the Erie between Utica and Syracuse.

[18]Howells, pp. 40–41.

[19]Taylor, Transportation Revolution, p. 52. See map, p. 35.

Problems of Structure, Approach, and Documentation

The paper will be more helpful as a sample if some of its underlying structural problems are examined. These may not be apparent just on reading it; the more nearly those problems have been solved, the less apparent they will be. One of the problems was making the secondary sources and the primary sources work together. The student tried to let his secondary sources interpret the primary sources and supply context for them. You will have seen that the first three paragraphs depend almost entirely upon secondary sources, and that they are intended as background for the subsequent discussion of primary sources. The central signpost of the paper does not come until the sixth paragraph.

Occasionally a reference to a secondary source comes into the discussion of the accounts by Hawthorne and by Dickens as interpretation or substantiation. But all the references to secondary sources together do not fully indicate the extent to which the writer used his secondary material. His reading of secondary material enabled him the better to select from his primary sources and to decide what material in them was most useful to his purpose.

The handling of his primary sources was not always easy for the student writer. (By this time you have discovered that your primary sources are not written with your convenience in mind!) In particular, Dickens' account of a canal boat journey is discursive, and handling it posed not only a problem in selection, but a problem in provision for a clear order of discussion as well. The student's treatment of each of his major sources was partly determined by its nature; he devised a pattern of discussion for each source as he worked with it.

The writer hoped that what is parallel in his two major sources would emerge clearly without his continual insistence. He also assumed that anything both writers remark is representative, and that it deserved his attention. There may be more extended quotation than is desirable; the writer thought that he needed to quote in order to give his reader something of the flavor of his sources.

The paper might have had numbered sections. If it had, where would the section numbers come? Would they be an improvement? The student writer thought his transitions clear, and that, in this paper, section numbers would be a distraction rather than an advantage to his reader. You should consider the transitions throughout. Sometimes there are no specific between-paragraph transitions. Is the relationship between paragraphs in those instances clear enough so that transition is unnecessary? The student rather fancied the major transition between the treatments of his major sources. Do you think it worked?

Documentation. If the student writer errs in his documentation, it is on the side of over-documentation. He has rightly used parenthetical documentation when he was dealing with the accounts by Hawthorne and Dickens: footnote documentation throughout would have resulted in a dismaying number of footnotes. Notice the footnotes establishing which editions of Hawthorne and Dickens were used. A volume number for *Mosses from an Old Manse* might have been given; since the book occupies a volume in the set by itself, a number is not necessary. The set of Dickens has no volume numbers. Footnote 11 is what has been called a supporting footnote. Footnotes 10, 12, 15, and 16 are documentation for statements which are made within the treatments of the accounts by Hawthorne and by Dickens, but which do not depend upon them. Footnote 17 has the rather special function of protecting the writer against any reader's supposition that he has overlooked an important matter in his sources. In footnote 19 a short title is used since the first reference to Taylor's book was made somewhat obscurely within footnote 17. The implication of the word "see" used in footnotes is that the reference is to an instance that supports a statement made in the text.

The student writer has been careful to identify his three primary sources in his text on their first appearances. Except in one instance, the names of writers of secondary sources are not mentioned in the text, since the secondary sources are used only for factual material, most of which might be found in a number of places. The one exception is the reference to Harlow by name, since he is quoted in the text, and since, so far as the writer knew, his is the best account of the Allegheny Portage.

appendix

Standard Reference Works

Your library will have scores of reference works. The following list of standard reference books, bibliographies, and special indexes may be a convenience to you. It is reprinted from *Heath's College Handbook of Composition,* 7th edition, but updated. Constance M. Winchell's *Guide to Reference Books* will supply information about the particular resources of reference books.

GUIDES TO REFERENCE BOOKS

Gates, Jean Key. *Guide to the Use of Books and Libraries.* 2nd ed. 1969.
Murphey, Robert W. *How and Where to Look it Up. A Guide to Standard Sources of Information.* 1958.
Russell, H. G., R. H. Shove, and B. E. Moen. *The Use of Books and Libraries.* 10th ed. 1963.
Walford, A. J. *Guide to Reference Materials.* 3 vols. London: The Library Association, 1966–1970.
Winchell, Constance M. *Guide to Reference Books.* 8th ed. 1967, and supplements.

GENERAL ENCYCLOPEDIAS

Collier's Encyclopedia.
Columbia Encyclopedia.
Encyclopedia Americana.
Encyclopaedia Britannica.
New International Encyclopedia.

GAZETTEERS AND ATLASES

Hammond's Contemporary World Atlas. 1967.
Rand McNally New Cosmopolitan World Atlas. Rev. ed. 1962.
Seltzer, L. E., ed. *Columbia-Lippincott Gazetter of the World.* 1962.
Shepherd, William R. *Historical Atlas.* 9th rev. ed. 1964.
Webster's Geographical Dictionary. 1969.

QUOTATIONS

Bartlett's Familiar Quotations.
Stevenson, Burton, ed. *The Home Book of Bible Quotations.* 1949.
Stevenson, Burton, ed. *The Home Book of Quotations.* 9th rev. ed. 1967.

ART AND ARCHITECTURE

Bryan, Michael. *Dictionary of Painters and Engravers.* 5 vols. Rev. ed. by George C. Williamson, 1964.
Encyclopedia of World Art. 15 vols. 1959-1968.
Haggar, Reginald G. *Dictionary of Art Terms.* 1962.
Hamlin, T. F. *Architecture through the Ages.* Rev. ed. 1953.
Myers, Bernard S., ed. *Encyclopedia of Painting.* Rev. ed. 1970.
Zboinski, A. and L. Tyszynski. *Dictionary of Architecture and Building Trades.* 1964.

BIOGRAPHY

Cattell, Jacques, ed. *American Men of Science.* 6 vols. 11th ed. 1965–1968, and supplements.
Current Biography. Monthly since 1940, with an annual cumulative index.
Dictionary of American Biography. 11 vols. and index. 1928–58.
Dictionary of National Biography. 22 vols, 1882–1949 and supplements.
National Cyclopaedia of American Biography. 1898–.
Webster's Biographical Dictionary. 1969.
Who's Who, Who's Who in America, International Who's Who, etc. Separate books containing brief accounts of living men and women. Issued more or less regularly.
World Biography. 5th ed. 1954.

CLASSICS

Avery, C. B., ed. *New Century Classical Handbook.* 1962.
Cary, M., et al. *Oxford Classical Dictionary.*
Harvey, Paul, ed. *Oxford Companion to Classical Literature.* 2d ed. 1937.

CURRENT EVENTS AND STATISTICS

American Annual. 1923–. An annual supplement to the *Encyclopedia Americana.*
Britannica Book of the Year. 1938–. An annual supplement to the *Encyclopaedia Britannica.*
Statesman's Year Book. 1864–. A statistical and historical annual giving current information about the countries of the world.
World Almanac. 1868–.

ECONOMICS AND COMMERCE

Coman, E. T. *Sources of Business Information.* 2d. ed. 1964.
Encyclopedia of the Social Sciences. 8 vols. 1937.
Dewhurst, J. F., et al. *Europe's Needs and Resources.* 1961.

Historical Statistics of the United States: 1789–1945. 1949.
International Bibliography of Economics. 1952–.
Moody's Manual of Investments. 1909–54. This series has been superseded by *Moody's Bank and Finance Manual*, 1955–; *Moody's Industrial Manual*, 1954–; and *Moody's Municipal and Government Manual*, 1955–.
Munn, G. G. *Encyclopedia of Banking and Finance*. 6th ed. 1962.

EDUCATION

Blishen, Edward, ed. *Encyclopedia of Education*. 1970.
Burke, Arvid J. and Mary A. *Documentation in Education*. 1967.
Ebel, Robert L., ed. *Encyclopedia of Educational Research*. 4th ed. 1969.

HISTORY

Adams, J. T., ed. *Dictionary of American History*. 6 vols. 1940. Supplement, 1961.
Bury, J. B., et al. *Cambridge Ancient History*. 12 vols. 1923–39.
Bury, J. B., et al. *Cambridge Mediaeval History*. 8 vols. 1911–36.
Handlin, Oscar, et al. *Harvard Guide to American History*. 1954.
Johnson, T. H. *Oxford Companion to American History*. 1966.
Langer, W. L., ed. *Encyclopedia of World History*. 4th ed. 1968.
Morris, Richard B., ed. *Encyclopedia of American History*. Rev. ed. 1970.
Sarton, George. *Introduction to the History of Science*. 3 vols. 1947.
Ward, A. W., et al. *Cambridge Modern History*. 14 vols.

LITERATURE – AMERICAN

Gohdes, Clarence. *Bibliographical Guide to the Study of the Literature of the U.S.A.* 3rd ed. 1970.
Hart, J. D. *Oxford Companion to American Literature*. 4th ed. 1965.
Kunitz, S. J., and H. Haycraft. *Twentieth Century Authors*. 1942. First supplement, 1955.
Spiller, Robert E., et al. *Literary History of the United States*. 3rd ed. 1963. Rev. bibliography supplement, ed. Richard M. Ludwig, 1964. This set includes extensive working bibliographies of major American writers.

LITERATURE – BRITISH

Bateson, F. W., ed. *Cambridge Bibliography of English Literature*. 4 vols. 1941. Vol. V, Supplement, ed. George Watson, 1957.
Baugh, A. C., et al. *A Literary History of England*. 4 vols. 2d ed. 1967.
Craig, Hardin, et al. *A History of English Literature*. 1950.
Dobrée, Bonamy, and Norman Davis, eds. *Oxford History of English Literature*. 12 vols. 1945–1963.
Harvey, Paul, ed. *Oxford Companion to English Literature*. 4th ed. 1967.

LITERATURE – CONTINENTAL AND GENERAL

Granger's Index to Poetry and Recitations.
Hartnoll, Phyllis, ed. *Oxford Companion to the Theatre*. 3rd ed. 1967.

Leach, Maria, and Jerome Fried, eds. *Funk & Wagnalls Standard Dictionary of Folklore, Mythology, and Legend.* 2 vols. 1949–50.
Mac Culloch, John A., et al. *Mythology of All Races.* 13 vols. 1964.
Preminger, Alex, F. J. Warnke, and O. B. Hardison, eds. *Princeton Encyclopedia of Poetry and Poetics.* 1965.
Smith, Horatio, ed. *Columbia Dictionary of Modern European Literature.* 1947.
Steinberg, S. H., ed. *Cassell's Encyclopedia of World Literature.* 2 vols. 1954.

MUSIC AND DANCE

Apel, W. *Harvard Dictionary of Music.* 2nd ed. 1969.
Gadan, Francis, et al. *Dictionary of Modern Ballet.* 1959.
Grove, G., ed. *Dictionary of Music and Musicians.* 9 vols. 5th ed. 1954; vol. 10, Supplement, 1961.
Sachs, Curt. *World History of the Dance.* 1963.
Scholes, P. A. *Oxford Companion to Music.* 10th ed. 1970.
Thompson, O. *International Cyclopedia of Music and Musicians.* 9th ed. 1964.

PHILOSOPHY

Boas, George. *Dominant Themes of Modern Philosophy.* 1957.
Copleston, Frederick. *A History of Philosophy.* 8 vols. 1946-1967.
Russell, Bertrand, *History of Western Philosophy.* 1945.
Urmson, J. O., ed. *The Concise Encyclopedia of Western Philosophy and Philosophers.* 1960.

POLITICAL SCIENCE

Bemis, Samuel F. *Diplomatic History of the United States.* 5th ed. 1965.
De Grazia, Alfred. *Politics and Government: The Elements of Political Science.* Rev. ed., 1962.
Political Handbook of the World. 1927–.
Smith, Edward C. and A. J. Zurcher, eds. *Dictionary of American Politics.* 2d ed. 1968.
Wright, Quincy. *The Study of International Relations.* 1955.

PSYCHOLOGY

Drever, James. *Dictionary of Psychology.* Rev. ed. by H. Wallerstein, 1964.
English, Horace B. and A. C. English. *Comprehensive Dictionary of Psychological and Psychoanalytic Terms.* 1958.
Harriman, Philip L., ed. *Handbook of Psychological Terms.* 1965.
Hinsie, Leland E. and Robert J. Campbell. *Psychiatric Dictionary.* 4th ed. 1970.

RELIGION

Buttrick, G. A., ed. *Interpreter's Dictionary of the Bible: An Illustrated Encyclopedia.* 4 vols. 1962.
Cross, F. L., ed. *Oxford Dictionary of the Christian Church.* 1957.
Ferm, Vergilius. *Encyclopedia of Religion.* 1945.

Hastings, James. *Dictionary of the Bible.* 5 vols. 1898–1904. Rev. ed. by Frederick C. Grant and H. H. Rowley, 1963.
Hastings, James. *Encyclopedia of Religion and Ethics.* 13 vols. 1908–1927.
Hebermann, Charles G., et al. *Catholic Encyclopedia.* 17 vols. 1907–22.
Jackson, S. M., et al. *New Schaff-Herzog Encyclopedia of Religious Knowledge.* 15 vols., and supplements.
Latourette, Kenneth S. *History of Christianity.* 1953.
Universal Jewish Encyclopedia. 11 vols. 1944.

SCIENCE

Gray, Peter, ed. *Encyclopedia of the Biological Sciences.* 1961.
Hawkins, R. R., ed. *Scientific, Medical, and Technical Books Published in the United States.* 2d ed. 1958.
James, Glenn, and R. C. James, eds. *Mathematics Dictionary.* 3rd ed. 1968.
Jenkins, Frances Briggs. *Science Reference Sources.* 5th ed. 1969.
Larousse Encyclopedia of the Earth: Geology, Paleontology, and Prehistory. 1961.
McGraw-Hill Encyclopedia of Science and Technology. 15 vols. 1960. See *McGraw-Hill Yearbook of Science and Technology* supplements to *Encyclopedia,* 1962–.
Newman, James R., ed. *Harper Encyclopedia of Science.* 2 vols. Rev. ed. 1967.
Thewlis, J., et al. *Encyclopaedic Dictionary of Physics.* 9 vols. 1962.
Van Nostrand's International Encyclopedia of Chemical Science. 1964.
Van Nostrand's Scientific Encyclopedia. 1968.

SOCIOLOGY AND ANTHROPOLOGY

Kroeber, A. L., ed. *Anthropology Today: An Encyclopedic Inventory.* 1953.
Social Work Year Book. 1929–.
Zadrozny, J. T. *Dictionary of Social Science.* 1959.

GENERAL PERIODICAL INDEXES

Readers' Guide to Periodical Literature. 1900–.
International Index to Periodicals. 1907–. Devoted chiefly to the humanities and the social sciences.
Poole's Index to Periodical Literature. 1802–1881; 1882–1906.
Book Review Digest. 1905–.
Essay and General Literature Index. 1900–. Contains author and subject index to collections of essays and articles.
New York Times Index. 1913–.
Ulrich's Periodical Directory. Classifies periodicals by the subjects they treat, giving a broad view of the magazine in the field.

index

The table of contents for this book provides a ready way of reference to the organization of source papers and the larger matters of form. This index is designed to allow you to check easily the details of source paper form and style.

Abbreviations

This listing of abbreviations includes those used in this book, with page references, and other abbreviations that may be encountered in source materials, with indication of their proper use.

cited" Sometimes (improperly) used to mean in the source cited.

MS, MSS   manuscript(s)

n., nn.   note(s) Used as p. 23 n; p. 102, nn. 6 and 7.

n.d.   no date Type with no space between, 8, 9, 46

op. cit.   *opere citato* "in the work cited" Formerly often used to stand for title in footnotes.

p., pp.   page(s) Not used when volume number precedes, 9, 45–46, 48

passim.   "throughout the work" or "here and there" Used as p. 21

et passim.

pseud.   pseudonym, 9

sic   "thus, so" Note that no period follows. Used in square brackets within a quotation to indicate that some abnormal form or spelling has been quoted exactly, 12

trans. (or tr.)   translator, translation translated by, 9, 48

v., vv.   verse(s)

vol., vols.   volume(s) Omit when volume and page number both appear, 9, 45–46, 48

Source Paper Forms and Style